LISTENING FOR LIFE

Cultivating the Courage to Connect

Patricia Taylor Johnson

26 25 24 23 22 21   1 2 3 4 5 6 7 8

LISTENING FOR LIFE: CULTIVATING THE COURAGE TO CONNECT
Copyright ©2021 Patricia Taylor Johnson

Unless otherwise noted, all Scripture quotations are taken from the New International Version of the Bible.

Names and identifying characteristics of people mentioned in this book have been changed to protect the privacy of those individuals.

All Rights Reserved. Except as permitted under the U.S. Copyright Act of 1976, no part of this publication may be reproduced, distributed, or transmitted in any form by any means, or stored in a database or retrieval system, without the prior written permission of the author and/or publisher.

Library of Congress Cataloging-in-Publication Data:
ISBN: 978-1-949758-99-3 Perfect Bound

Published by:
Emerge Publishing, LLC
9521 B Riverside parkway, Suite 243
Tulsa, OK 74137
Phone: 888.407.4447
www.emerge.pub

Cover Design by: Christian Ophus
Listening sets a bruised heart free.

DEDICATION

*To Bill Foster, VP of Spiritual Care, Trinity Health
Dennis Guernsey PhD, Fuller Theological Seminary
Fr Bernie Owens SJ
and Marilyn Keller, friend extraordinaire–
the four individuals who most
contributed to my spiritual growth, insight
and ability to listen.*

ENDORSEMENTS

Writing from the authentic perspective of a veteran healthcare chaplain, Pat Johnson unites with her readers as she demonstrates the art of basic human connection through listening. Accentuated with illustrations from her ministry, the author's approach invites us on a journey that is as introspective for her as it is other-focused on those for whom she has cared. Johnson infuses a wholly accessible spirituality throughout even as she induces our similar reflection in a meditative muse for faith seekers of all types -- *William Foster, VP of Spiritual Care, Trinity Health.*

An inside look at chaplaincy, the value of presence and how often showing up is the greatest gift we have to offer. A very readable how-to that touches both the heart and funny bone -- *Nancy Sparrow, Therapist and Spiritual Director.*

Pat Johnson starts with stories from her work as a chaplain, draws us into the wonder, awe and grace she experiences, and then offers ways to reflect on our own spiritual journeys. A gifted storyteller, she weaves together the world of the hospital and the world of the spirit, drawing us into God's presence through her own experiences, and with the questions she poses to us.This book can be read all at once, or you can savor each section, using it for reflection, journaling and prayer. The author's experiences mirror our experiences of fear and worry, connection and faith. and she leads us reliably toward God with her writing -- *Mary Austin, author of Ashes at the Coffee Shop, Resurrection at the Bus Stop, Senior Pastor, Gaithersburg Presbyterian Church.*

Pat Johnson has redefined what it means to listen. Her fifteen years as a hospital and hospice chaplain have brought an awareness, understanding, and sensitivity to a way of being that most of us are thirsting for - to be heard, to be listened to, with kindness... something we need more than ever in the midst of the pandemic. Pat draws back the curtain of this most important life skill and touches our hearts in the process -- *Micky Golden Moore, Chaplain and author of Tails Beyond the Pawprint: Twenty-Two Stories of Love, Loss, and Lessons Learned from our Adored Animal Companions.*

TABLE OF CONTENTS

Introduction   ix

1	Suspending Judgement	1
2	Everything is in Process	7
3	Heart to Heart Access	14
4	The Courage to Enter	21
5	Who You Know	28
6	Breaking the Cultural Barrier	34
7	Listening for Commonality	44
8	God of the Unexpected	54
9	Let God Be the Judge	62
10	A Tiny Window of Opportunity	72
11	An Angel's Touch	80
12	Changing Landscapes	87
13	The Great Equalizer	93
14	Two Perspectives	100
15	Medal of Worth	108
16	Losing Control	115
17	The Power of Validation	122
18	The Still, Small Voice	128
19	Of Patience and Connection	133

20	Erasing Life	140
21	The Power of Presence	147

Epilogue: Our Mark	157
Acknowledgements	161
Notes	163

INTRODUCTION

Everyone appreciates being listened to. It is a rare gift to give a person who simply wants the attention of another person—full and uninterrupted attention (no looking beyond the person, no slyly checking the watch or cell phone, no preplanning what to say next). Think about how many times in your own life you have ached for that kind of attention, that kind of listening. Most of us go to therapists for that. We seldom find it anywhere else.

I am a healthcare chaplain and have had the privilege of journeying alongside a vast array of people—the wise and the foolish, the searching and the self-sufficient, the humble and the proud. I have listened to many people devastated by grief or loss of function, pain, addiction, mental illness, dementia, or generalized life confusion. This has been my ministry for more than fifteen years.

There have been times when I felt my work was ineffective and a few times when I would have rather been doing something else. For the most part, however, I have savored every day, looked forward to pulling into the hospital parking lot, saying a prayer that God would walk with me throughout the day. Even on days when I felt sleepy or lacked energy, I usually left at the end of the day feeling energized and at peace. Some days, I left carrying a burden for a patient or family but had to learn how to let go of the weight so I could be present to my family and refreshed for the following day.

In every situation of coming alongside patients and their families, I have discovered one immutable truth: Everyone benefits when true listening happens—especially the listener.

Why do you think therapists are such good listeners? It began with a love for people and wanting to help them. It usually evolved into getting the extra training to fully utilize what was most helpful in a conversation with another person (along with a truckload of theory and statistics!). But everyone can benefit from learning how to listen well.

My intention for writing this book is to offer you an opportunity to bypass all of the education, classes, and clinical education I have taken to learn so much of this. I have attempted to translate it into accessible everyday language.

Perhaps you want to make a difference in another person's life, but you wonder how to do that beyond the practical meeting of needs (which is important, but not the only thing the other person needs.) Showing up in another person's life is the first step, and it is a huge step in our increasingly busy world. Listening to someone you care for—not to fix a problem or respond with "me too,"—but listening deeply with your focus on the person in need adds so much more.

Listening brings about better relationships. Listening to another person can also help you go deeper into yourself, sorting through your own thoughts and feelings. It can bring people and families together instead of driving wedges between them. It is not a quick fix, but it can deepen relationships and communicate how much you care by giving the other person time and room to share what they need to. Too often, we are uncomfortable with silence, with waiting. We jump in before the other has a chance to really think about what they want to say.

True listening brings empathy into a conversation. When you truly understand what another person is communicating, your own judgements, opinions, and defenses disappear. You begin to relate to the other person deeply and empathetically. You feel their pain, their fear, their frustration. And you care more about them than you care about yourself in those moments.

Many of us lose our bearings in relationships. We don't know what to do to make things better. Our insight is lacking, and we become discouraged. We read books on communication. We listen to self-help podcasts thinking that if we just apply a formula, it might be the magic that fixes the problem. Or maybe we blame the other person for the lack of relationship because we believe that *they* don't listen to *us*.

This book will provide you with insights and practical examples into what it takes to really listen. Each chapter is divided into three sections: a listening story, my discoveries within the story, and personal reflection questions for you to ponder. Some of these questions may require that you take some time to think about your own circumstances. There are no right or wrong answers, only the answers you discover for yourself. But the time invested will give you fresh perspectives and highlight what you could do differently with God's help. Remember, as we give of ourselves to others, God gives wisdom to us—almost simultaneously. It is a matter of having open hands and an open heart, not prejudging, not needing to have the last word. You will end up listening for life and growth in the other person, and you will listen for the same within yourself.

When you reveal to another that you are vulnerable and open, the tendency is for them to follow your model. This does not mean that you put all of your own "stuff" out there, but at appropriate times, you might share something in your own life that makes you just as human as the person you are caring for. At these times, you also get to model how you "pick yourself up, dust yourself off and start all over again" (a well-known quote from an old popular song used by a veteran of Weight Watchers). You can admit your mistakes and maybe even humbly ask for forgiveness.

I promise you that when you begin to listen more intently to others, to yourself and to God, your life will change. You will discover what I mean by listening as you read through the stories in this book. You might say, "These examples don't apply to my life." And my response would be: "Really? You never encounter difficult people, confused people, angry people, misjudged people?" Think again. Start listening for life.

My hope is that the examples from my life and experience will give you a bit of insight into how this might be done (or not done on occasion!). And my prayer is that you will grow and change by the act of listening intently and intentionally to others.

God bless you on your journey!

When someone deeply listens to you
it is like holding out a dented cup
you've had since childhood
and watching it fill up with
cold, fresh water.
When it balances on top of the brim,
you are understood.
When it overflows and touches your skin,
You are loved.

—John Fox, Finding What You Didn't Lose

CHAPTER 1
SUSPENDING JUDGEMENT

"...the nun's habit can also give younger members a dangerous sense of security, of being special, separate, elevated to a new level of holiness automatically without doing the long, hard, tedious work of conversion."

—Kathleen Norris, *The Cloister Walk*

On my first overnight, I donned my lab coat like a nun's habit, knowing I was entering a sacred space, one that I wondered if I had any right to occupy. We were encouraged as chaplain trainees to see ourselves as pastors. But to me, based on my history, a pastor was someone who was 1) male, 2) holier than me and 3) inaccessible. To see beyond this stereotype, to call myself "pastor," would take time and a shifting orientation, seeing myself from a different vantage point.

The resident chaplain, Raj, had been assigned to train me during that particular overnight. We spoke briefly before taking the elevator to the first floor Emergency Room. My perfectionist tendencies were kicking into hyperdrive. I wanted to know everything about everything all at once and nail it down. Chaplaincy isn't like that. It's a free-flowing responsive interaction with whatever comes your way...not something that came naturally to me. Poor Raj.

Not only did he have my training stretching out before him, but he was on overnight duty himself—except that while my overnight was five hours long, his was twelve. On top of that, he had a hospital-wide service to lead via an internal television network the following morning.

He escorted me into the ER (emergency room) at 10 p.m. We were notified that a trauma patient was on her way. In the interim, we began to visit patients. "Hi, I'm Raj, one of the chaplain residents, and this is Pat, who also is a chaplain. We will keep you in our prayers."

I moved from bed to bed with him, holding hands with each patient and washing between visits with a non-drying hand foam to curtail the spreading of germs. (My hands took on a reptilian quality as we inched closer to dawn.)

I soon learned I had to be myself. While Raj felt fine speaking to each patient in a repetitive way, I did not. I am a hand-holder. Inwardly, I was chiding him for being so distant. Outwardly, I smiled and moved on. I had so much to learn...

The patient we had been waiting for finally arrived at the ER and was hurried into the trauma area. I tried to stay out of the way, fading into the background and looking to Raj for cues. Our trauma patient had suffered third-degree burns from a gas explosion in her home and was here for stabilizing before being transferred to a local burn center.

She entered the room on a gurney groaning softly as the medical team moved into action. I was amazed at the synchronicity of their movements, each knowing exactly what to do and when. They made few comments. She was severely burned—her arms, legs and torso—over eighty percent of her body.

Raj took me by the elbow into the hallway, moving me into the family waiting room. The patient's sons and one daughter-in-law were seated in the room looking dazed. "I just can't believe this happened," her eldest said. "I just left her a few hours ago…"

I was expecting Raj to say something, but he only nodded and listened. These were my early days when I thought that I had to come up with just the right words at just the right time. I wondered why he wasn't taking charge of the situation.

The patient representative entered from the hallway. (This is the person who keeps track of the who, the what, and the where of the patient—a central communication point for all involved in serving the patient.) "Your mother has serious burns over most of her body," he relayed to the family members. "We will be moving her to the burn center shortly."

I sat with the family, mystified. How does one cope with the uncertainties? What goes on in the mind of a person suffering from shocking news like this?

I, of all people, should have known. Several years ago, my youngest son had been involved in a rollover accident and brought to this very hospital. He had been taken into the trauma room and placed on the gurney next to the one this woman now occupied. I had been sitting in the very seat in which the eldest son was now sitting. I had been waiting to hear if our son was dead or alive.

What *did* that feel like?

I remember reaching deep within myself for shelter from the action around me. Did I remember what anyone had said to me? No. What I *do* remember is a kind face moving into the room and asking me if there was anything we needed. "Yes, please call our pastor. Here is the name of our church…" He had taken it down and quietly moved out of the room, returning a few minutes later to tell us that he had left a message. No one answered. There was no forwarding or emergency number.

When we could finally see our son, we were relieved that he was conscious. He suffered many injuries—spleen, lungs, ribs, ankle—but he was alive and would be fine if the doctors could expand his breathing capacity and stop the internal bleeding.

These thoughts swirled within me like a tornado touching ground and then lifting. What I saw before me was a family as traumatized as the patient, although in an emotional rather than a physical way.

When the ER doctor walked slowly into the room with downcast eyes, I knew that the news was not good. "Your mother did not make it. Her burns were too severe. We will not be moving her. I'm sorry." Raj expressed his sympathy and once again waited for the family to respond. He sat with them, an immovable presence within a swiftly moving, seismically changing world. They talked. They cried. They began the litany of "What ifs?" They made phone calls. They closed their eyes. They cried some more. I observed.

Raj left the room to find out when the family could say goodbye to their mother. I glanced at each person in the room. *What do I do now? Is there something I can say that will help? Maybe pray? Probably just sit still and see what happens...* Raj came back shortly and told the patient's family that she was ready for viewing.

"Would you like to say goodbye?" he asked. We all rose quietly. Each son had his arm around someone, and they slowly walked into a small room adjacent to the trauma room within the ER. There was the patient, her mouth propped open with some kind of depressor, her arms limp at her sides. Her family hovered over her, wanting to touch her and not wanting to touch her, afraid to leave, afraid to stay. "Would you like me to say a prayer?" Raj gently inquired.

"That would be nice," her daughter-in-law responded between sobs. Raj prayed for the family. "And be with this one who is now in Your Presence. Amen." *How does he know that this patient is in God's presence? And how can he pray this way without knowing more about the family?* Raj already understood the expansiveness of God. "Bidden or not, God is present." (Desiderius Erasmus)

What I did not understand then—but do understand now—is that Raj was letting God be in control. While Raj held to his own theology as a solid foundation for his life, he was allowing God's Spirit to minister freely to this family and patient without any preconceived notions about what was right, appropriate, or just. I was surprised, and I pondered this deeply within my heart. *Love...is kind...is not proud...is not self-seeking...always protects, always trusts, always hopes, always perseveres...*" (1 Cor. 13:4-7). Rather than quoting scripture, Raj *embodied* scripture, unselfconsciously, freely, graciously.

The family finished their good-byes. As they were walking down the long hallway to the outside doors, they turned to us. "Thank you so much." They hugged us both, then they left.

Job descriptions within the hospital are delineated by color of dress. Dark blue means one thing; light blue another. Those in burgundy are ancillary. White lab coats are reserved for professionals: administrators, doctors, chaplains. And so, by donning the white lab coat, I was making a statement. *I am a professional. You can count on me. I am trustworthy...an expert.* After that experience with Raj, however, I came to the conclusion that my coat should have been green. *I am a newbie. I don't know what the heck I'm doing. Look out! I might do or say something incredulous!* We were trained to acknowledge and respect the vulnerability of patients, but truth be told, I felt as vulnerable as any of them in my new role. However, I was determined to earn the right to wear that white lab coat and all it represented!

God on Both Sides of the Equation

Here was a family who endured a major life event and who were principally in shock. Little did they know what this evening would bring to them. They cried, they held one another, and they left with gratitude on their lips.

What was it like being new? I was tentative. I realized I had to let go of my perfectionistic tendencies. Delving into the "real me," I knew I could not emulate Raj. I also knew I could not tell God what to do or how to do it. I was learning humility.

In the silence, I was learning how to listen and had to set my "fixes" aside, realizing that there *were* no fixes. Learning to be comfortable with silence was not new to me since I had had training in spiritual direction. In that context, silence was a friend. It gave each person time to respond from the depths of their spirit instead of drawing from the surface.

This was a new setting, and my fear and discomfort pushed me into thinking that I had to *say* something. I was re-learning that listening does not always require me to respond verbally. Sometimes the non-verbal communication is more powerful. Listening in this way also allowed me to learn how to suspend judgement, to withhold preconceived pigeon-holing of a person, especially one in need. I was learning that embodying my faith was more important than talking about it. In the trauma of the moment, I was learning that God was the one ministering through me, and simultaneously, God was giving me an object lesson.

Listening to Your Heart

- When trying to help someone, have you ever felt that you had to have answers? Were you trying to come up with the answers instead of listening to the other person's pain?
- How comfortable are you with silence? Do you find yourself trying to fill in the gaps in conversation?
- What would being silent, not sharing answers, feel like to you?

CHAPTER 2
EVERYTHING IS IN PROCESS

"Help me, Lord, to be content with process, not just product. Spiritually, I will never see a finished product until I see You face to face. All of life—its stages, ebbs and flows—is process. There is a perpetual reaching, moving, unbinding, retreating; everything is in process..."

—*Patricia Taylor Johnson*

Sometimes the most intriguing, comical, and meaningful encounters happen late at night. Hospital staffing is lighter. Things usually happen at a slower pace. There is more time to think, respond, and reflect.

A nurse paged me at 1:30 a.m. one night. She sounded exasperated as she requested a priest. "Is the patient dying?" I asked.

"No, but he asked for a priest," she said.

"Well, I am not a priest, but do you think he would still like a visit?"

"Absolutely!"

I realized after the fact that this was *her* response to the question, not the patient's.

She then told me that the patient had been brought back to his room by security. He had been constrained from leaving the hospital on his own to stand outside and smoke. He had wanted to talk to someone about his frustrations.

Her page had roused me out of a sound sleep. I set the receiver down, slipped on my shoes, my lab coat, and badge. I walked into the restroom provided to sleeping residents and chaplains and peered into the mirror. Any bed hair, goopies in corners of eyes, unexplained wrinkles caused by sheets or blankets? All looked as good as it could—as far as I could tell. I opened the door, slipped out and headed for the elevator. As often happened at this late hour, I was in the elevator alone. I could have been praying. I should have been praying. Instead, I was trying to open my eyes enough to look awake, jumping up and down to get the blood flowing, singing quietly to exercise my voice, and shaking my head from side to side to initiate brain action. Did it help? I wasn't sure!

I rode the elevator up and then walked out and over to the north wing. As I rounded the corner, I noticed a middle-aged man walking toward me, grasping his IV pole on wheels, fully dressed and looking very intent. His nurse had her arm around him in a very protective way. "There's the chaplain!" she chirped to Mr. C. "And here is the man who wanted to see you!" She aimed her announcement in my direction.

"I just wanted to smoke. I needed to talk to you. It was underneath, you see. I ain't too sure." *Great,* I thought. *An incoherent patient, probably in detox.* My eyes brightened. *He probably won't even notice how tired I am!*

"Why don't we go back into your room and talk?"

"OK." I followed him into his room and walked to the far side of the room by the window. Another patient lay in the bed that I had passed, but the curtain between them was closed, and he appeared to be asleep.

"Is this private enough for you?" I inquired.

"Oh, sure." He sat down on his bed and looked up at me. "I just can't get the estimate. They're trying to do this thing. It's around and under here. I'm scared of the tests." The corners of his eyes crinkled as he winced.

"George, may I call you George?" I had noticed his name on his wristband.

"Sure."

"George, I need to go out of the room for a moment. Please stay here and wait for me right where you are."

"OK."

I walked back to the nurse's station to speak to the woman who had called me. "Can you tell me something about George's medical problems?"

"Sure. He's in here for ETOH." She gave an acronym I did not understand.

"What is that?"

"Alcohol detox. He's been a real problem tonight. You saw the security when you walked up here?" I nodded. "They had just brought him back. He tried to go outside to smoke. It's been one of those nights..." I looked at her sympathetically, remembering how frequently I hear people complaining about hospital care, but know that those same people never hear about how tough it is to work in a hospital.

"Thanks for the information." I walked back to George's room and stopped by the foot of the bed.

"Father, I just wanted to get out of here to smoke, "he said." It's backwards, and I'm not sure of it. It's slipped under something. Father, it's OK. Father, I just want to leave."

I desperately tried to follow his train of thinking, but it seemed derailed.

A voice from out of nowhere penetrated the curtain pulled between the two beds. "George, we've both been in the Marines, and Marines don't leave each other—ever!"

I poked my head around the curtain to see the other patient sitting up in bed. Could he possibly see the look of gratitude in my eyes? I'm thinking, *an angel, disguised as a patient...*

"George, can I pray with you?" This usually has the effect of settling patients down, unless, of course, they don't believe in God. I knew God was already in the room, but I really needed to connect with God at that moment on behalf of George.

"Yes, please, Father." Don't think for one minute that his term was lost on me. I'm thinking, *Do I tell him I'm not a priest? Am I being truthful here?*

I prayed for him, focusing on his anxiety and fear, and then we said The Lord's Prayer together.

"I have some tests today—an endoscopy and colonoscopy—and I'm scared." George revealed.

"That's tomorrow, George. Not today," The voice from the other side of the curtain interjected.

"You know the tests are necessary so you can get better. The doctors need to know what's going on so that they can help you."

"I just want to go outside and smoke, Father."

"That's not going to be possible. You have to stay in here so you can get better."

"Yes. Father." He hesitated and then said, "I know you're not a Father, but I feel better calling you that." He reached down, grabbed my hand and kissed it. *Being all things to all people certainly took on a new meaning for me that night!*

"I know. It's OK. Now this is what I want you to do: Put on your pajamas and get back into bed and get some sleep. Promise me you will not try to leave again." Sometimes a "Fatherly" approach is exactly what's needed.

"Oh, I never lie to a priest. I won't try to leave, Father." He began to remove his jacket and change into his pajamas so that he could climb back under the covers. I averted my eyes.

"I'm going to leave now, George. You'll do as I asked?"

"Yes, I will."

I left George and stood by the bed of the other patient. "Hey, thanks for helping out tonight."

"No problem. You know, he was fine until the nurse came in, even asleep. Then he kind of went bonkers."

"Thanks again," I sighed. "I hope you can get some sleep now, too." I left the room and returned to the nurse's station to relay my prognosis.

"I think he's going to be OK now. He's getting ready to get back into bed and try to sleep. If he gives you any more problems, please page me again."

"Thank you *so* much. It's been a really rough night." Her bloodshot eyes revealed her fatigue. "We've had two patients wandering the halls tonight. I think I need to find a nice, quiet closet and sleep."

"Is there anything I can do to help *you*?" I asked.

"No, but thanks for asking. I'll be OK."

A couple of days later, I arrived at the hospital for rounds. As I walked through the revolving door, I looked ahead. There was George, walking sheepishly between two guards, being escorted back to his room. I don't think he saw me. If he did, he responded by looking down and away.

God on Both Sides of the Equation

George and I were both learning the ropes. Sometimes it means taking a step backward before we can take two steps forward, understanding our place in a larger context, getting rid of preconceived notions, trading comfort for truth, and being easy on ourselves when we revert back to old habits of thinking, acting, and relating. It's all part of the learning process of allowing God to use me as I partner with Him.

There will be times when my presence and my listening appear to be of no avail. I gave it my best effort, and the results were apparently the same as they were before I entered the picture. Does this mean God does not use my efforts? I don't believe this. I am one piece of a very large human puzzle. I cannot afford to miss opportunities to be with and listen to others simply because my interventions seem to be worthless. Who am I to judge? Being present to a person is not about solving a problem but being part of the ongoing process in a person's life that I do not need to fully understand.

Is it ever OK to ignore a person's misconception of me? I have to weigh what does the most good or harm. If I had corrected George, I might not have had the opportunity to spend time with him. Yes, he was confused, but he also knew the truth. There are appropriate times when we think outside the box, breaking "rules" for higher purposes. We know the rules, and then know how to creatively break them!

George was angry and frustrated. How can I listen to his complaints without taking it personally? It involves getting some emotional distance and not being defensive or trying to solve the problem. Some would call it thick skin. Sr. Jose Hobday calls it "gospel skin." I believe that it has more to do with where my focus is. Is it how I feel or how the other person is feeling? Can I get myself out of the way long enough to really hear, listening to what is being said underneath the anger?

You might notice that I checked in with the RN. She is also a caregiver, and caregivers need as much, sometimes more, support than the patient. I try not to be oblivious to those surrounding the patient and sometimes fail when my focus is too intense on the patient's needs. It helps to think, "Who is part of the caring circle for this person, and how can I support them as well?"

In a quite remarkable way, George's roommate was *my* support– a very unlikely candidate. He was allied with me in the cause, and I deeply appreciated it.

Directness and firmness, done with compassion, are sometimes very necessary, but risky. As people who love other people, we do risk a lot by being directive. I use this cautiously and not very often. It takes a great deal of trust to initiate this kind of entry into a person's heart.

Listening to Your Heart

- How do you handle the discouragement of attempting to help someone by listening and caring apparently to no avail? Is it possible that your discouragement speaks more about your own needs rather than the needs of the person in front of you?
- Do you usually have a need to correct someone when they make a wrong assumption? Would it help or hinder your relationship?
- Reflect on your own history with anger. How might this knowledge affect your being a presence to an angry person? Are you able to get emotional distance and see beneath the anger?
- What helps you trust another person? What hinders you?

CHAPTER 3
HEART TO HEART ACCESS

It is not a small gift of His love, this opportunity to be offered upon the sacrifice of service—something you would not naturally choose, something that asks more of you than you would naturally give. So rejoice! You are giving Him what He asks you to give Him: the chance to show you what He can do.

—Amy Carmichael

One of the most amazing things about being a chaplain is the doors it will open for me. Just today, I was on the phone with a local women's clothing store trying to convince them that the 50 percent coupons I had given my sister as a "thank-you" gift for putting my husband and me up at their home in Tennessee were valid.

"You were supposed to keep them stapled to the receipt," she chided. "Can I trust you?"

Okay, *now*... "Well, I'm a chaplain... and if you can't trust your chaplain, who *can* you trust?"

"That's good enough for me." I could visualize the smile stretching across her face.

"Are you sure you don't need the store number where I bought them or anything off the receipt?" I offered.

"Nope. We're good."

See what I mean? Being a chaplain does sometimes make life easier!

My first night rounding in the Intensive Care Unit Tower had a bit of that mystery about it. Every door was "openable" by card, badge, button, or voice. As I entered each double door on every floor in the tower, I had a sense of power, thinking to myself, "I can go anywhere in this place—unrestricted access."

Little did I realize at the time that unrestricted access also means opening myself up to the shuddering recognition that I lacked the ability to solve all problems those vulnerable people presented to me. I was also opening myself up to a tremendous responsibility—to learn how to *be* with anyone who asked.

We underestimate this gift of simply "being." In our culture, we feel obligated to suggest answers. We may agree with someone assigning guilt. We verbally champion risks taken. Then we try to say something helpful or exit gracefully when there is nothing left to be said.

Prior to my hospital chaplaincy, I had worked in a children's hospice. Late one afternoon, the hospice team received a call to meet a mother in the Emergency Room at Children's Hospital. Her baby had just died. Our team had developed a relationship with her over the past year and wanted to see her through the crisis.

When I walked into the ER, she was sitting on an examining table holding Harvey in her arms, his legs dangling onto her lap. She rocked back and forth as if attempting to sooth him. Grandma, a thin, elaborately accessorized Black woman, sat on a chair across from her, frowning and groaning, "I told you not to give him those medications. That's what killed him." The mother's sister was sitting on the table next to the mother, rubbing Harvey's head.

"What kind of a God answers prayer like this?" Grandma spit out. "I fully expected him to be healed." She got up and walked out. I gave her plenty of space to do so.

The hospital children's chaplain was gently pressuring the baby's mother, Shirley, to allow her to take Harvey's footprints as a memorial, a way to preserve his personhood after he was buried.

Somehow, I felt as if I had no business being present. And yet, Shirley and I had talked about faith and doubt, healing and resurrection, and a myriad of other topics. I had followed her around the city on my monthly visits. One time I listened to her as her legs hung out of the car she had been living in after having been kicked out of her mother's home.

What in the world did I have to offer her on that day? I offered to pray, which she received as we held hands with one another—a small, sad circle of love and support. After the prayer, I sat down next to her and put my arm around her. The doctor came in and out, the family shifted position—standing and then sitting. The children's chaplain left her paper and ink pad on the cart after asking me if I would suggest to Mom that she take a picture of her baby and get his footprints. I just couldn't do it. It seemed sacrilegious. It seemed like something to do when there was nothing to do.

I sat for the longest time just touching her and then looking into her eyes, the saddest, biggest brown eyes I have ever encountered. We locked gazes, and then she looked away. She knew. I knew. There was nothing left to say. She had lost her baby—the baby we had prayed for that God would have mercy and heal him. His soft, warm absence left a crater in her heart—one that she did not even yet recognize was there, she was in such shock.

As more family arrived, I excused myself to allow them to grieve in private. The hospital sent in their grief representative, the one who attends to making arrangements. My job was done.

In my hospital internship, accessibility meant being present at the death of an elderly man undergoing heart catheterization, standing in the background next to the nurse who ran the high-tech monitors searching for any sign of life. I watched the doctors attempt to revive him. I watched them complete their job on a lifeless body. Then I moved outside the surreal cockpit of the operating room into the waiting room to sit with the family until the doctor came in to tell them he had died on the table.

Accessibility meant stumbling around in the dark at 3:00 a.m. in the sleeping room, fumbling for my glasses, checking my face for mascara smudges, wetting down my hair and trying to walk a straight line down the hallway to the trauma center. It meant tending to a woman who had brought her baby in through emergency after he had been bitten by her boyfriend. This is how he took out his revenge for her ending the relationship.

Accessibility meant sitting with a middle-aged woman watching the monitor as her mother slowly died after suffering a massive stroke. "Wouldn't you like me to turn that off?" the nurse gently offered, as soothing as a hug. "No, I want to see when it happens," she replied. We sat side by side as I listened to her recount the events of the day, having had no idea that this is where she would be at the end of it. Her mother had seemed fine when she left the assisted-living facility earlier in the day. And then the call came. The staff nurse called an ambulance, and she had been taken to the hospital. When she arrived, it was too late. She was already actively dying.

"Is there someone you would like me to call?" I asked.

"No, I am the only one who lives close by, and I've already called my brother who lives out of state."

"May I get you something to eat or drink? You look tired."

"Just a glass of water, please."

I left the module for a few minutes and returned with ice water. I sat down next to her again as we watched the numbers on the monitor slowly drop. It took several hours. I left occasionally to attend to other patients and families. When I returned, I sat down next to her as the lines went flat and the numbers disappeared from the screen.

"Can you read something from the Bible?" she asked.

"Of course." I chose a passage in 2 Corinthians 5 and ended with "...therefore, we are always confident and know that as long as we are at home in the body we are away from the Lord. We live by faith, not by sight... (so we) prefer to be away from the body and at home with the Lord..."

I sat on a chair by her side and held her hand. We sat for many minutes until the nurses came in and asked her if she needed more time with her mother. She nodded, and they left. I stood up. "You may want to be alone with your mother. I'll come back and check on you."

She nodded again, and I closed the curtain behind me. It was late, and I stood up against the wall outside of her curtained cubicle in the ER and felt as if I had been holding it up. But I knew in my heart that God was the one holding *me* up...

Twenty minutes later, I pulled the curtain open noiselessly and walked into the cubicle. She stood, faced me and reached out her arms for a hug. We embraced, and I silently prayed for her. She gathered her things and turned to start the long walk back to her car in the emergency parking lot. I stopped her for a brief moment.

"Would you like me to walk with you?" I offered.

"No, thanks. I'm OK."

I walked her to the hallway and watched her as she made her way to the Emergency Access Only door. She opened it with a touch of her palm and melted into the darkness that was occasionally punctured by streetlights.

As she walked, I reflected on the idea of access. Yes, I had access, but it didn't bring power. Instead, it brings us face to face with our weaknesses. It causes us to huddle together, share our humanity like a shawl. We touch one another and many times, without realizing it, we release the power of grace into one another's lives.

God on Both Sides of the Equation

Access into a person's soul brings with it the revelation into our own vulnerabilities and inadequacies. I had a greater responsibility to learn how to *be* with people in pain. I also had to learn how to give people space when they needed it, and that involves listening, really listening to what their needs are in the moment. I came to the conclusion after many encounters that I should never discount feeling like a "fly on the wall." Presence is always a gift and one that might give access to a person's inner life of thoughts and feelings down the road.

When the baby died, I wondered what on earth had I really done? Because of *access*, I was present. What does "being present" really mean? We had had a history of sorts to fall back on when words were inadequate. The power and presence of God hovered between us, *and* within us. God did what neither of us could do, reaching down within each of us and giving us exactly what we both needed. We might or might not have been conscious of it, but that did not diminish what was happening as I looked into her eyes. We lived in that moment alone.

It is also true that allowing a person to tell their story to you without interruption or judgement really helps the person telling the story. The woman who waited for the monitors to announce her mother's death shared what the day had been like for her. She had an opportunity to take something indescribably painful and put it into words so that it could drift down into reality for her.

And then there is the healing power of touch. It can confirm that listening has taken place. It might be a thank-you hug or an I-just-need-someone-to-hold-me-up kind of hug. Touching can break down barriers, connecting two very different people and bringing harmony into being just when it is needed—a multi-layered song that blossoms out of pain. There are those who would rather not hug but who need to be alone or just need a simple presence (which, many times, is not so simple for us!)

Holding a person's hand can be just as intimate as a hug. Looking into someone's eyes can be a form of listening. It says, "I am here for you, and I am listening to your heart."

Listening to Your Heart

- What does it mean to be present to someone? How do you convey presence? How does it feel on the inside? What might it look like on the outside?
- Have you ever been present to a person but did not know what to do so you just stood there? How could you reframe that experience so that you acknowledge the power of presence?
- How could you encourage someone to share their story with you, especially when you now know how important that can be?
- Learning how to "read" a person is like listening. Do you have any examples of doing this with those you love?

CHAPTER 4
THE COURAGE TO ENTER

"Despite what we know about spiritual growth, nearly all churches in America are characterized by an unwillingness of members to commit themselves deeply to their respective church. For some it means church hopping; for most, it means keeping the church at arm's length— that is, living as if the individual's life is primary and that of the church is secondary."

—*Joseph Hellerman*

Whenever patients ask me what my denomination is, I always reply, "non-denominational." That seems to satisfy their curiosity for the moment. Besides, the visits I make are not about me. *Or are they?*

Certainly, I am rarely asked to engage in any deep esoteric theological points. Most patients are more interested in the answer to the question, "Does *anybody* really care about *me?*"

I have always believed until recently that being non-denominational made me more available and accessible to more people. I read about, attended and studied the gamut—charismatic to Anglican,

Congregational, Lutheran, Covenant, Missionary, Presbyterian, Community, Methodist, Episcopalian, Catholic—and I considered myself to be eclectic, borrowing from this tradition and that, picking through and tripping over doctrine to arrive at something that I like to call simply Christian.

Apparently, these days, it puts me in company with a variety of individuals who have been burned, shut out, disappointed and/or scarred by their selected congregation. Many middle-aged patients, when asked about their ties to a faith community would reply, "I don't attend church...anymore. I used to, but that was before_____ (fill in the blank).

I feel for them. I really do. I know what it is like to suffer through unresolved misery in a church only to feel as if leaving is the only thing that will give me peace. Sharing wounds did not feel possible, and I felt unable, because of tandem hurts, to make myself vulnerable enough to entrust my thoughts and feelings to many people. The ones I did share with were usually the ones who had already decided to leave for a variety of reasons.

And then came the search for a new church home. First, I avoided looking since my time was given over to seeing that my mother had the best care possible in assisted living (and failing at it numerous times). I had no energy left to invest in new relationships. So, I put it off. My husband and I had our own devotions at home. That was safe. And I believe that, at the time, it was OK, especially with God. God knew what we were going through and kept us very close.

When we did venture out, we drove quite a distance to a downtown church that felt nurturing and used liturgy, which I grew deeply attracted to along the way in my spiritual journey. Being "surrounded by such a great cloud of witnesses" (Heb. 12:1) appealed to me. I felt connected generationally to millions of believers on the earth and over time. Liturgical worship gave me a sense of community, if you will, albeit invisible or virtual. Having lost my father fourteen years previously and my mother more recently, and with my only sister living out of state, I yearned for connection.

The drive downtown became prohibitive over time. Sundays were fine, but weeknights became impossible, and my need for community remained unmet. We then decided that perhaps the mega-church that opened a satellite a few miles away from home might be the answer. I was not thrilled with the lack of liturgy or silence, but agreed to make a genuine effort to "plug in." A few years later, I still felt disconnected, even though I had given myself over to several ministries in the church on a limited basis. Our small group was spread out over a thirty- to forty-mile radius. We saw each other Saturday evenings, but that was about all.

We finally ended up at a congregation less than a mile from home. The congregation spanned several generations, had liturgical services and sermons that were short and deep. We decided to give community a chance to encircle us, wounded as we were the last time we ventured into one in depth.

I cannot say that we did not grow while we searched and traveled and sat still. But growing deep and growing wide are two different things. I believe God calls us to grow both ways. One feeds the other.

So, while I saw my non-denominationalism as an asset, it was also a liability. This came into focus when I encountered a patient who was being treated for severe asthma. When I entered her room, she was stretched out in the bed, fully dressed and laughing.

"Hi, you look like you might be leaving today, "I remarked.

"Well, I sure hope it will be today or tomorrow! I'm feeling so much better." She grinned from ear to ear.

"That's good to hear! I'm stopping by today to see how things are going for you and to tell you a little bit about our services."

"OK."

"We visit all patients in the hospital to address their emotional and spiritual needs. Our services are available 24/7. (This is a pretty challenging statement. It has to be heartfelt and individualized, and speaking it thirty or forty times a day with conviction can be tough!) I noticed on my computer printout that your religious preference is blank. Would you like me to fill in your faith tradition?"

"Well, I used to be Catholic, but I'm not really practicing anymore." *How many times have I heard this?* Not just from Catholics, but from Episcopalians, Lutherans, Baptists, etc. "I went to Catholic school but just don't feel like it fits me anymore. I'm open to pretty much anything these days. I guess you could call me an atheist. I don't usually tell people that. Most people don't like to hear it."

"Mmmmm... I imagine that's probably true." *Why is she sharing this with me? Is it because she feels comfortable with me or because she wants to get my attention?*

"In fact," she continues, "I went to a restaurant recently and saw a fortune teller. I paid $3, and she told me things you wouldn't believe!

"When my father died, I kept a lot of his things. I put them in a drawer in a secretary in the living room. The fortune teller told me that someone was looking after me, and she said that person's things were in a drawer in my living room. I couldn't believe it! She said she can get this information from the energy coming from people. I guess she must be gifted that way."

"That's very interesting. How did you feel about her insight?"

"Oh, I felt great. I left her feeling so good, too. You know, I don't attend church, but I still believe. My children were raised Catholic but when they were older, I let them make their own decisions."

"And what did they decide?"

"Oh, they decided to stay with the church. I sometimes go with them to the Shrine of the Little Flower. I mean, it's OK, but it doesn't do anything for me. I just don't believe in the institutional church. I'm a good person, and my children live good lives, too."

"You know, sometimes the church has a hard time communicating what it really needs to be communicating. Faith has so much more to do with a person's relationship with God, not conformity with rules and structure," I said.

"I really believe that! You are so right!"

As I turned to leave, I wondered if I had really been faithful to what I knew—that searching for just the right church has a lot to do with our need for community, not just our own personal journey. That God works in context as much as he works in the one-on-one. The disconnectedness and discomfort that I was beginning to experience as I walked out the door was magnified by this patient's incongruities and spiritual confusion.

Just this morning I had an opportunity to speak with my son who called me from an assignment in India. He has had his own broken journey with the church. "I don't really care too much about going to church," he said.

"Then why are you talking about visiting a church when you return from India?" I inquired.

"Oh, I don't know. I'm going to give it one more chance. I believe in God, and that seems like enough most of the time, but I feel like I need to be around people, you know, to be with them... I just can't tolerate, though, the shallowness I once did. It's got to be better than that or I'll give up once and for all."

Shortly after I hung up the phone, I sat down and read these words from Kathleen Norris' book, *The Cloister Walk*. "Not long ago, I was asked by a college student how I could stand to go to church, how I could stand the hypocrisy of Christians. I had one of my rare inspirations, when I know the right thing to say, and I replied, 'The only hypocrite I have to worry about on Sunday morning is myself.'" She then goes on to mention the "profound hospitality of Cecil Williams, the pastor of Glide Memorial Church in San Francisco, who insists that "the church is not just for believers." In his book about the church, *No Hiding Place*, he says simply, "When people come to Glide, we don't ask them if they are atheists, Methodists, or Buddhists. We ask them what their names are and how they're doing...On Easter Sunday (I) invite people to tell their own stories during the service. One year, (I) said, 'There's an empty tomb somewhere in this room this morning. I invite you to come forward now.'"

How do we share our own stories if we have no one to share them *with?* What makes me think that I can function just fine solo even though God is in community in the Trinity and a choir cannot be composed of just one voice? Even a soloist needs backup singers to create a fuller, more meaningful sound. Then there's the adage about a tree falling in the forest. If no one hears it, does it really happen?

God on Both Sides of the Equation

Sometimes listening to another person deeply can bring our own needs to the surface. This is not a bad thing. In fact, it helps us identify with the other person. It is not something, necessarily, to share but to contemplate and bring to God at a later time. If we commented on our own thoughts and needs, we would be taking the focus off of the other person and placing in on ourselves. The outcome of the encounter would be very different.

Was I really in a place to help this person even amidst my own confusion and winding journey? I need to keep asking myself, *Am I getting in the way of ministering? Am I distracted because of my own problems and issues?* This is a time to set those aside, put them in God's hands and give your full attention to the person in front of you. You might be very aware of your own inner turmoil, but you need to put it on the back burner in that moment.

If you find that the voices in your head are screaming at you and are louder than the person's voice in front of you, it might be time to schedule a second encounter after you've had time to search and identify the source of the noise in your soul. This is something you and God can do together. Sometimes it helps to have a good therapist as well.

Why do some people open up so easily when they have been burned for doing so before? Sometimes, when I show interest and concern to a person, the floodgates open just because I am showing interest and concern.

Do you have any idea how seldom a person is really listened to? For some, it might be never. Maybe they are overbearing. Something as simple as being overweight keeps people at a distance. Or hair that hasn't been washed in a week. Maybe they even smell bad. Perhaps the person is depressed and those in her/his life are tired of hearing about it. Maybe the person has a difficult time hearing, and others are not fond of shouting. There could be a myriad of reasons that someone never receives a good "listening." Then I walk in, ripe for the picking and usually very glad to allow it.

What can give us the courage to enter into a listening mode with a person? I believe it all has to do with God's love flowing through us toward that person. There have been days when I really didn't want to be with people. I didn't want to listen, but I went out on the floor anyway. Those were some of the very best encounters I have had simply because *I* got out of the way and allowed God to do His work through me!

Listening to Your Heart

- When was the last time someone opened up to you in a way that brought your own journey to mind? What did you do in that moment? Was it helpful?
- Are there certain people or types of people that you consciously or unconsciously avoid when you set out to care for and listen to people? Have you been able to allow God to work in you to change your perspective? What might it take?
- How open are you to attending to conflicts within yourself? How might these conflicts help or hinder those you are caring for?

CHAPTER 5
WHO YOU KNOW

*"It's not **what** you know; it's **who** you know."*

—Anonymous

Today, a friend who I have known my entire life is being buried at a local cemetery. Her funeral was yesterday, a nagging reminder of the speed at which life is traveling.

Julie and I were fifteen years apart in age. My first clear memory of her was as my Sunday School teacher when I was eleven or twelve. She was *scary*—demanding, persistent, expecting much and giving much. I was timid, maybe more into Beatles than Beatitudes, but there was something about her that was solid, faithful, and consistent. She was never afraid to speak her mind even when it was inconvenient or embarrassing.

As the years passed, I grew to love her, trust her. Somehow, she decided to invest in me. Many of her friends could say this very thing, but she made me feel like I was the only one. I remember many, many late-night dinners at her house, talking about Jesus until after 2:00 a.m.

I recall sitting with her at the little booth in her kitchen holding her youngest daughter, the baby who was born years after her first three girls. I was married by then, and up to that time, I had been unable to conceive. She put her hand on my arm and said, "God is going to give you a child." And I thought, *Well, that would be wonderful.* But she *knew.* Eleven months later, I was holding our first-born son.

Jesus was at the center of everything for her, and those who knew her, knew this. She was one of only two people in my life (the other being my husband) who had no interest in small talk. She wanted to talk about God; she wanted to talk about Jesus and His kingdom.

After my husband and I moved to Los Angeles where I attended seminary, her calls came at frequent intervals. Even when I was out of her sight, I was not out of her heart. And I know that she faithfully prayed for me over the years as well. God knows I needed it!

Years later, after we moved back to the Midwest, came the monthly breakfasts—her gift to her friends—a place to be loved, cared for, and a place for sharing and receiving the deep things of God.

One late night at the hospital, I printed out my list of Emergency Center patients as was my routine. I always scanned the list first to get an idea of what was coming my way. There on the list was my friend Julie. Knowing how much she hated hospitals and doctors, I was shocked to see that she had been brought into the EC. I donned my lab coat, checked its pockets for all of my necessary paraphernalia—list, pens, pocket Bible, key to the sleep room, tissue, gum, debit card, and lists of meaningful verses. Closing the door behind me, I strode to the EC a little faster than usual.

When I entered her cubicle, two of her daughters were present, as well as her sister. They had brought her in because she was unable to swallow. After I checked in with the family, a patient representative pulled me aside and said, "By the way, there is a patient here who was just told she has thyroid cancer, and it doesn't look good. You might want to check in with the family." I looked up at him with sadness in my eyes. "I already have. She is one of my best friends."

"I'm so sorry," he said softly.

None of her circle of friends and family could believe this was happening to her. She was the nurse nutritionist. She was the strong one. She had taken care of herself so faithfully over the years. And now she was the one with the grim diagnosis.

I was in training at the time and had been reading a book called *Practicing the Presence of People: How We Learn to Love* by Mike Mason. He shares the story told within Federico Fellini's film, *8½*, about its own making, about a director in search of a script. Guido, the director, attempts to put a script together, but as he cannot put his own life together, so too is he unable to pull together this film. Throughout the making of the film, he encounters grotesque-seeming characters from his own life. At first, he believes *he* is the "normal" one, and the others are alien. He then realizes that "he, too, is lonely and estranged, involved with these people but not connected to them, cut off not only from others but from himself."

"Guido cannot make a film about himself because he cannot accept his life as it is… that he himself is no better or different than the relationships he has formed. The sum and meaning of his life is not to be found in (his) art, but in people. The people he knows—all of them—these *are* his life."

The director does not emerge from his isolation until he is able to join hands with his cast, a part of his own show, and be at one with his own people. The title of the film refers to his shoe size. He does not "fit" until he puts on this circle of people like a pair of old, comfortable shoes.

As Guido, I carry all of my relationships with me as I encounter others. Without the people I've had around me my entire life, I would be an empty shell, feeling isolated and wondering if my life had meaning. We all have experiences that change us and mold us, and many of these changes are due to the people who have entered our lives.

Before I began my rounds in the EC for the evening, I stopped by Julie's room. Her initial diagnosis had been confirmed by a biopsy. She had thyroid cancer—the worst kind and very invasive. It had already spread throughout her upper torso and had wrapped itself around her esophagus which is why she was having a difficult time swallowing.

I prayed with her, cried with her, read her scripture, and held her hand. When I left her room, a chaplain friend was waiting outside the door. I held out my arms to him and told him I needed a hug. He obliged, and then I told him why. That's one of the wonderful things about chaplain colleagues! They know how to comfort.

I left her floor and began my rounds in the EC. In Module A, I came across a woman in her 40s, an attorney, who was inebriated and had taken drugs earlier in the day to numb the pain of her life. Her mother had died in her 50s. Her father had committed suicide. Her brother had gotten into a fist fight with her—on her birthday—and here she was in Emergency, numbed and bleeding and bruised. She told me she was a "lapsed" Catholic.

I listened to her and stroked her forehead, pulling the hair out of her eyes. I told her that she was in good hands and that God loved her and wanted to reconnect with her. She marveled at the gentle care she received and promised to go back to church. Her friend, who just happened to be named Julie, had called her that very day to wish her a happy birthday and to encourage her to return to her faith. We prayed together; I held her hand. I don't know for certain if she will even remember our conversation, but I do know that God will not forget her or her promise to return to God.

As I reflected upon these two encounters, I realized that I am who I am because of the relationships with which I have been graced. Julie, my friend, was always there for me. This young woman in the EC benefited from my connection with Julie (and her Julie). I joined hands and formed a circle—my Julie on my right and this patient on my left. Because of our interconnectedness, we shared in the sufferings of humanity *and* in the grace of our Father. With Mason I can say, "In the end, who (I am) is who (I) know."

God on Both Sides of the Equation

I feel utterly alone at times. I know most human beings have this feeling on occasion, and I know it is usually fleeting. During those times, I am sometimes reminded that there is a rather long queue of people who have passed through the doors of my life and have given me something rather special. I am, after all, part of a larger community—even with those who are no longer alive. I sometimes forget this.

It is an accumulation of life experiences and people who help to shape our identities. For some, the shaping is lopsided and irregular, needing to be reshaped by the tenderness of others. Such was the case for this patient. I, on the other hand, have had quite a bit of nurturing in my life. Part of being a human and a Christian is recognizing that what we are given is not ours alone. It is to be shared and sometimes given away. This is how God works in His economy. If what we have is never shared with others, be it material goods or solid relationships or positive experiences, we can grow brittle and protective. God cannot permeate into our souls when we are like this. It's almost as if there is a roadblock in our soul.

It's not required we share all of what we've been given when we are in a helping mode, but it does help to have these things brought to consciousness. Hoarding our privilege, if we are so blessed to have it, must be disdainful to the God who gave so much to us. Realizing that what we have is to be given away frees us to be part of the circle of love that can surround the person who desperately needs it.

Listening to Your Heart

- What gifts has God given you to use and to share? When you are caring for someone who needs what you have, are you even aware of it? How might you become more aware?
- When you listen to the life of someone who has given so much to you, are you able to discern his/her impact in your life? How might you pass this along?
- Do you think your time and effort are wasted on those who might not be able to fully experience your love—as in the case of the woman who was inebriated? How can you combat this false view of the use of your gifts?
- Can you think of a time when you were surprised at the effect you had on someone in a seemingly insignificant encounter?

CHAPTER 6
BREAKING THE CULTURAL BARRIER

...you were the flame; you were the sacrifice and for those few hours, the heat of your little life melded our lives together...

—*Patricia Taylor Johnson*

There is something about partnering with an idea in the abstract that is heady, powerful, and almost romantic. I became a hospice chaplain on April 9, 2007. In preparation for this honorable profession, I read everything I could get my hands on that had to do with death, mourning, bereavement, and anticipatory grief. I handily organized and re-organized my files once I arrived at the cozy cubicle I would call my office space. I wrote task lists, checked them off when completed. I listened to others lament over what might be, what probably would be, trying to refine my listening skills. I eased into my self-induced projects with gratitude and glee.

Then I met baby Jorrell. I knew him for only ten hours, but in his presence, I could not escape the reality I had been preparing for—a reality that was more startlingly real than I imagined it could ever be.

I was on a retreat with my fellow chaplains and had been easing into a contemplative state of mind. This was a special retreat for it demanded nothing of us except to rest and allow God to minister to *our* spirits, which is often a sorely neglected task in the life of a chaplain. We were given scripture to meditate on and were encouraged to go for a walk on the grounds of the retreat center. It was an oasis in the middle of lives that were buried in listening, grief, and necessary paperwork. As I got up to leave, my cell phone rang. It was the children's hospice physician. My first patient when joining the hospice team was dying. Could I go to the housing project and be with the family?

"Of course! I'll be there as soon as I can," I replied. I got into my car and began the journey from the suburbs to the inner city where our offices were located. Jorrell's mother's apartment was approximately two miles from the office.

When I arrived at the housing project, I was let in by a man who was ranting about someone threatening him, someone evil who had been challenging him. He muttered so much under his breath that I could not quite catch everything he was saying (not only do I strain sometimes to hear the subtleties and inflections of inner city Black dialect, but I am also a bit hard of hearing in my right ear, and he happened to be on my hearing deprived side.) I had seen him walking down the street when I got out of my car. When he opened the door of the project, I hoped he was headed the other way.

"It's so evil out there," he continued. "I done seen things..." When he stood by the elevator talking with me, I boldly responded (not exactly knowing what I was responding *to*) that it is the Light that overcomes the darkness. He continued to talk in circles, but when we reached the 8th floor, I stepped out of the elevator, and he thanked me for ministering to him.

I looked back and forth between two long hallways, one to my left and one to my right, wondering which way to turn. I chose left incorrectly, unable to find the number I was given on either side of the hallway. Discovering my mistake, I turned around and headed the opposite way, glancing down at the carpet and the walls that appeared to be a construction project in process. At that point, I was not into the details since my mission was to find Jorrell's apartment and offer solace to his family as he lay dying. When I found the right apartment, I used the knocker to announce my arrival.

The door opened, and I looked behind it to see a woman of enormous girth holding it open for me. "I'm here to see Keesha," I stated. "Over there," she pointed. I was not quite prepared for what I saw. A young, *very young*, beautiful and thin, Black woman sat on the black textured loveseat next to a couch of the same color and design—a teenager. And beside her, lying on a blue protective pad was Jorrell, who appeared to be struggling for breath. I introduced myself to her, placed my hands on Jorrell's head and silently breathed a prayer for him.

As I looked around the room, there were numerous individuals in a variety of positions around the room—some were standing, some sitting, others kneeling. Most were young. I made the rounds checking to make sure everyone was doing as well as possible under the circumstances. An older woman sat on the arm of the sofa, and I noticed a cross around her neck. I approached her and asked what the cross signified. Since crosses are worn by people of faith but also by those of no faith whatsoever, I take no chances assuming anything anymore. She told me she was a Christian. Since it was a crucifix, I offered, "Catholic?"

"No, Baptist," was the reply. Without any preface or invitation, she launched into the story she kept close to her heart. "My thirteen-year-old daughter died." It was more like an offering than anything else. I made some appropriate comment about her being able to identify with the mother whose baby was dying, about her being a source of comfort to the teenager.

"Are you related?" I asked.

"Oh, we're just friends, real close—like family. Keesha's like a daughter to me." She then pointed out her birth-daughters, two of them among the assorted individuals in the room. As she explained who was who, I knew I would never get it quite right and was irritated with myself for not having a better memory with names, faces, and relatedness.

Kneeling down in front of Jorrell, I stroked his arms, his legs, his head. He was pudgy but handsome. Dr. Jean was sitting next to him wiping his mouth with a 4x4 gauze pad. The blood was bright red and continued to ooze from his mouth. I recalled hearing the words at one of our meetings, "bleed out," and wondered if this was what I was seeing. The doctor looked up at me with a sympathetic look. The plastic bag at her feet was half full of the same brightly stained 4x4s.

Part of our job as a team is to bring comfort to the family, to make death as pain-free and palatable as possible. I could see that for the young mother, a teenager who had never seen death up close and personal—at least not *this* personal, we were not being successful. She turned away often and actually left the room more times than I could count. A few times, she actually left the apartment. I could not imagine not holding my dying child, but I am in my fifties and have already seen death up close and personal. I have never found it distasteful or unmanageable. That's probably why I'm in this business, and she's not. I tried hard not to blame her.

The hours went by. At times, time moved rather quickly. At other times, the minutes congealed, refusing to budge. The hospice nurse, the physician, and I took turns with Jorrell since he needed constant attention.

In the early evening, I passed the torch to the physician and spent a few moments outside on the balcony far above the street. It was a very hot, muggy day. The horizon looked as if a grey shroud had been wrapped around its shoulders, the pollution of the city settling upon its buildings and skyscrapers. I knew it was important for Keesha's mental health that she spend some time with her son. How was I to move her from the bedroom to the living room where his little body lay dying? Sometimes directness and honesty, if delivered with love and compassion, is the best solution.

I walked into the bedroom and sat down beside her. "I can't even imagine how difficult this is for you," I spoke quietly, hardly above a whisper. She stared straight ahead as if she had not heard me at all. I placed my hand on hers and continued, "Your son needs to hear your voice. He knows you, and he will find it comforting to feel your hand on his body and hear the love coming through your words to him. Please think about this. It's so important right now."

What a tough thing to ask a fifteen-year-old! She sat on her bed, completely numbed out by what was happening. I asked her to do something so far beyond her years, it was almost incomprehensible.

I left her sitting on the bed having done what I thought would be helpful, not only for her baby but for her own peace of mind when she will recall that moment years from now.

Returning to my sentry position on the balcony, I watched an ambulance drive swiftly by. Its driver may be only faintly aware of attempting to stem the tide of death that threatened to enter another home and wash over another sad family.

As I turned to re-enter the apartment, I saw Keesha bending down beside Jorrell. I prayed a silent prayer of gratitude. God had given her strength of spirit to face what no young woman should have to face. I could hear her softly singing, not quite catching the words. When a person approaches death, hearing remains acute until the very end. I knew Jorrell could hear his mother's voice, and what baby would not be comforted by that?

Dr. Jean asked if I could handle this on my own until the nurse arrived. She was already on her way, and she had to stop by the hospital to see another patient. I could see no reason why not.

I continued to swab Jorrell. The sun had set, and darkness was enveloping the city. The nurse arrived twenty minutes later. I noticed that Jorell's chest expanded only slightly and erratically. Bending down, I spoke softly into his little ear. "It's OK, Jorrell. It's OK to go now."

Within an hour, his breathing had stopped completely. The family and friends moved into mourning mode, and the funeral home was called. The physician returned to pronounce him deceased and noted the time of death on his certificate. When the station wagon arrived to take his body to the funeral home, Keesha's older friend, the one who had lost her daughter, gathered him up in a blanket and carried him down the stairs to the outside of the building. After gathering our things, cleaning up the living room and making sure the family was cared for, we followed her and surrounded her as she placed his body on the gurney. The driver strapped him down and pushed the gurney up against the back of the trunk, its legs bending to allow him to push it in.

As we were standing huddled together on that late muggy night, someone threw a glass bottle at us from a window far above. We were startled by its breaking on the concrete, shattering the sacredness of that moment. I walked to my car and made the long, silent drive home.

―――

Days later, I so wanted to make sense of what I had experienced. It was the first patient death of my career, and I knew it would set the tone for the rest of my ministry to patients and their families. I was finally able to write out the meaning that I drew from this event in the form of a poem.

Patricia Taylor Johnson

Jorrell

On a sultry,
sullen autumn evening,
we watched, from your balcony,
a waning house fire
smoking in the distance
as if now at ease
puffing its tension
into the air.

You lay at rest,
your last exhaled breath
drifting heavenward
out of labored lungs,
the tension of choosing—
life or death into life—
finally resolved.

We waited hours
for your release,
watching the flames
of your little life
dwindle and then rekindle.
We were fooled
several times into
thinking that the fire
within you
had truly exhausted itself—
smoke and ashes
left behind.

But you surprised us with
a re-ignition
now and then
to let us know
that your fire would
only be extinguished
when *you* decided to
let it go out.

And so,
we waited,
crouched in the
humanness of waiting,
souls combusting,
sharing hours that
would never have
otherwise been shared,
sharing secrets that
would never have
otherwise been whispered.

When Love was truly enkindled
among us,
a fusibility between
age, gender, color and creed
prevailed.
You left and
left behind
an incense,
a last ascendable breath
that brought us together
in the unlikeliest of
places and times...
you were the flame;

> you were the sacrifice
> and for those
> few hours,
> the heat of your little life
> melded our lives together.
>
> Now we are
> forever changed,
> burning more brightly,
> more beautifully,
> because of you.

God on Both Sides of the Equation

The most challenging thing about caring for Jorrell and his family/friends was that no one volunteered to speak with me. We were cultures and lifetimes apart. They didn't know me. They only knew what they saw and heard. They might have even been rightfully suspicious of me. I had to set these feelings aside to do what I came to do—to extend love and support to each one of them as well as Jorrell's mother and baby Jorrell himself.

How can I listen when no one speaks? Well, there are always the non-verbal cues to be aware of. Who seems to be in need? Who displays openness? Who needs comforting? I may read it correctly or I may not. I cannot take it personally if I attempt to reach out and find rejection on the other end.

One way I try to ignite a conversation is to notice something about a person, showing interest in something about them. I noticed the cross hanging around a woman's neck. When I asked about it, she was open and very willing to share about it and her own experience of loss. This gave me an opportunity to listen and love her. There was no one else in the room who spoke up after that. I had to be content with silence and presence (which are not to be undervalued).

Choosing to gently request that Jorrell's mother attend to her son was risky. Being directive is sometimes important. I have had a patient family member push me away or shove me against a wall when I attempted to gently comfort or confront them. Of course, this pushing away happened when I was very, very green and in some ways, didn't know any better. I wasn't reading the person accurately. My intuition has improved with experience.

I was so grateful that she eventually honored my request and sat with Jorrell, speaking and singing to him. At the time, I didn't know what the outcome of my intervention would be. I just took a chance and prayed that God would use it for His good. And He did!

Listening in this context was more about noticing and then listening to God's Spirit within me so that I "did no harm." I also knew how important it was to listen to myself and attend to my own needs after the event. Depletion is never a good thing when one cares for another. By writing a poem about the circumstances surrounding Jorrell's death, I was caring for my own soul, listening to its needs. Writing was a salve on the deep wound that opened up in me that day.

Listening to Your Heart

- How comfortable are you with silence? Even silence that might be fraught with suspicion or fear?
- Can you recall a situation in which you noticed something about a person in a group and commented on that something? Was it helpful to encourage the person to open up? Why or why not? If nothing comes to mind, try this and notice what happens.
- How do you feel about taking a risk with a person who is already very vulnerable?
- Do you listen to yourself and take measures to care for your own needs when you care for others? How?
- Remember, it's not about you. Be vulnerable yet tough enough to take risks.

CHAPTER 7
LISTENING FOR COMMONALITY

"It is amazing how much love and laughter (dogs) bring into our lives and even how much closer we become with each other because of them."

—*Josh Grogan (Author, Marley & Me)*

A couple of weeks ago, I sat mid-way down on the basement stairs crying my eyes out. My husband and I were in the middle of a rare argument. There seemed to be no resolution to our dilemma. We were stepping gingerly through the country of feelings—the invisible yet valid world of emotions—unseen and powerful. Hurtful when shared with an edge to the voice. I sat crumpled and wondered how we could ever understand one another. And then it happened.

Two of our rescue dogs padded quietly down the stairs after carefully walking around my husband who stood on the landing. One of them went to the bottom of the stairs and stretched out on the carpet. The other stopped on the stair where my elbow was holding up my head, and he pushed into me. Oh, I could read so much into this—have a virtual field-day with his intentions—but the very fact that he came and nestled in close to me spoke volumes. I was in need, and the dogs were present. What else is there to say?

During my first two units of Clinical Pastoral Education at the hospital, I probably saw close to 7,000 patients as I did my rounds and responded to emergencies. I was amazed at how many people talked about their dogs. Being admitted to the hospital or waiting several hours in Emergency creates another kind of emergency with dogs. Who will let them out? Who will feed them? *Did* the person assigned to the task remember to do it? Is the dog stressed by my not being home? Who will give the dog his medication? And on and on and on, enough to stress out the healthiest of us, let alone those of us who are sick or injured.

I remember quite vividly a dog owner who happened to be on the Orthopedic floor. When I looked into the woman's room, she was sitting in a chair looking rather discouraged. By reading her chart before I entered her room, I learned that she had an infection in her right knee that was not responding to the antibiotic she was being given. Previously, she had fallen and broken her femur just above her artificial knee. An infection had set in after her surgery for the broken femur. She had already been in the hospital for a week, which is longer than normal for this kind of condition.

I introduced myself to her. "How are you today, Ms. J?"

"Oh, I'm OK." She seemed a little hesitant to talk with me, so I decided to probe just a little bit more.

"You look a little down."

"Well, I've got a long haul ahead of me. I'm going to rehab in the hospital first and then to rehab at a facility." She shook her head as if in disbelief. There was more there than met the eye. Patients assigned to hospital rehab usually had more medical problems than the ones being treated in off-site rehab and needed to be more closely monitored.

"Did you have a knee replacement?"

"Well, it's a little more complicated than that. I broke my femur just above my previous knee replacement, and so they had to fix that. Then they had to reattach the bone somehow to the prosthesis."

"I see." I nodded.

"I really miss my dog." As she shared this with me, she looked into the distance as if she could actually see her dog.

"Oh, what's his name? Do you have a picture?" I moved in a little closer. Since I have three dogs of my own, we began an instant bond.

"His name is Ivan. No... I don't have any pictures with me."

"What a cute name!"

"Thanks! He's a Chihuahua/terrier mix—you know, like the Taco Bell dog except with a bit more fur. He's been shuffled around from house to house so much lately since I've been in here."

"Wouldn't it be nice if he could be here with you?" A dangerous thing to suggest. I was weighing the pros and cons as I said this to her. *Would the extra possibility of infection be worth the extra emotional undergirding a dog would bring?*

"Yes, he loves sleeping with me."

"My dogs sleep with me as well. One of them especially snuggles up to me tightly. It's hard to even roll over!"

"That's Ivan! I have this entire queen bed to myself, and he sleeps so closely to me. I'm already right on the edge. If he pushed a little more, I'd fall out!" We laughed picturing this together.

"Have you thought of calling him? Dogs love to hear our voices."

"I didn't think of that! That's a great idea! I'll call him tonight!" Her smile, once tentative, began to broaden. "You know, I did that one other time when I was away, and he got really excited."

"Non-dog people think we're crazy, but we don't care, do we?" We were really together in this!

"Not at all!"

"It makes him happy, which then makes *you* happy."

"That's such a great idea. Some people are cat people. I used to have a cat, but there's nothing like a dog!"

"That unconditional love—they never care what we look like. We can even be in our pjs all day, and that's fine with them." I was opening the door a little wider, hoping that we could move into a spiritual direction.

"Yes. He's such a sweetheart! You know, I think God gave us dogs to be with lonely people—to keep them company. I don't know what I'd do without Ivan. My children are all grown. They have their own lives now."

I stood there impressed at how she so quickly got to the heart of things!

The dog theme came in handy for me a few weeks later. As part of our training at the hospital, we were required to lead two services per unit. These services were broadcast over the hospital network as they took place in the chapel on Sunday mornings so the patients who desired to tune in could do so from their hospital beds. Whether people sat in the chapel or not, we led the service as if the room was full. I was in charge of the morning service on one particular Sunday. I turned on the monitor and cable hook-up and began by introducing myself and praying. Next came the scriptures for the day. It was at this point that I began the homily (a mini-sermon.)

As a writer, I have always been told to write about what I know. So, it follows that sharing a homily should be the same. This is what I shared after I read the gospel passage for the day, which was Matthew 22: 34-40:

> "Hearing that Jesus had silenced the Sadducees, the Pharisees got together. One of them, an expert in the law,

tested him with this question: 'Teacher, which is the greatest commandment in the Law?'

"Jesus replied: 'Love the Lord your God with all of your heart and with all of your soul and with all of your mind.' This is the first and greatest commandment. And the second is like it: 'Love your neighbor as yourself.' All the Law and the Prophets hang on these two commandments."

I don't know about you, but when I read this passage, I find that I do understand the second commandment, loving my neighbor—I'm not always successful at it, but I usually understand what it means and what I am to do.

However, when I read the verse that echoes the first commandment, "Love the Lord your God with all your heart and with all your soul and with all your mind," I take a step back and wonder how I can love God. The Word tells us in I John 5:3 "This is love for God: to obey God's commands." This is true, but how do I show God that I love Him by keeping His commands and not feel as if I am simply following a set of rules?

Why would we even consider loving God? I John 4:19 says, "We love God because God first loved us." Our love is in response to God's love. If we do not understand or accept God's love for us, we will have a difficult time loving God. So then, what does God's love look like?

Recall the parable of the prodigal son in Luke 15:11-24. When the father saw the son coming, he was filled with compassion and ran to his son, threw his arms around him and kissed him. That is what God's love is like. How do I feel about someone who goes out of his way to run to me, seek me out, who throws his arms around me? Who loves me no matter what I think, feel or do? In spite of what I've done? Yes, the son had made a decision to return to the father and by reading the passage, we cannot be certain that he wasn't manipulating the situation, perhaps even strategizing, but the father did not wait until the son was in front of him, begging for forgiveness. *The father ran as soon as he saw the son coming.*

I'd like to share with you a little story from my own life that brought clarity to the meaning of God's love and how I can love God back.

A few months ago, we adopted a rescue dog…a little Bichon Frise named Sidney. We had picked him out by looking at pictures online. When we found out that he was rescued from a "puppy mill," we at first balked, wondering if we should take on a dog with "issues." When being interviewed by the agency (yes, they interview people who adopt dogs—in fact we had three interviews and *they called our vet to make sure we would make good owners), we were encouraged to try a "puppy mill" dog. They are, of course, harder to place.*

Sidney arrived on a Sunday afternoon at the local airport. He was in a little crate and very frightened. We took him home and loved him up as best we could, but he was so wary, he backed off from any movement toward him. We made it through the first night—two anxious adults and two anxious dogs. (We had another Bichon named Beaumonde. Sidney was brought home to be his friend.) The following morning, as my husband was opening the door to get the paper, Sidney slipped out. He ran so fast… we were amazed. It took six adults (we recruited my son, his friend and two neighbors who were out walking) to find him, hunt him down, and corner him. Forty-five minutes of near misses by people driving on their way to work, doubling back several times, an "almost got him" moment… two cars and at least two of us in slippers with cowlicks in our hair. It was, after all, 6:45 a.m. My husband in one car, my son in the other finally cut him off and cornered him into a backyard, half a block from the main highway. You can only imagine what would have happened if he had made it to the highway during rush hour!

The most relieving words I heard that morning were, "We have him." We brought him home, dried the dew from his body, held him and sat down in the living room staring at each other for at least half an hour. "Can he ever run!" "I would have never guessed that such a quiet, timid little dog could outrun four of us and two cars!" "I'm exhausted! And the day hasn't even started yet!"

That night, I was alone with both dogs as my husband went to work that morning to an out of town location. I readied the bed and plopped both dogs up on the end of the bed. Sidney was tired... no wonder! However, at about 2:00 a.m., I awoke to the sound of howling and crying. I felt so sorry for him. He was in a strange place with strange people and strange smells. He had been in foster care for six months and now was having to start all over again.

I gently lifted him beside me and began scratching his tummy. He relaxed just a bit but still cried out. I then began to sing to him, "Amazing Grace." Good thing I had several verses memorized... I sang to that little dog for four hours. And as I sang, I began to weep, realizing in a profound way, that I am like Sidney in so many ways... and God goes after me, hunts me down, and sings to me because he loves me, treasures me.

How then do you think Sidney felt after that night? He followed me around like he was glued to me. He got excited at the sound of my voice. When I drove up in the car, he began wagging his tail. He would walk so close to me that sometimes I tripped over him. He wanted to be with me. He loved me.

Think about it. When you can come to the realization of how much God loves you, what God has done to take care of you, how God has visited you when you were down and dirty, rebellious and in pain, you cannot help but love God back. For it is in receiving God's love that we are able to love back and then to love others even when they may be as unlovable as we were when God first approached us. When God finds us, we are forever changed.

The first commandment is to love the Lord with all of your heart, soul, and mind. And the second is to love others as you love yourself. The very first step is accepting the love God has for you—as you are—where you are at this moment.

A few days ago, a young man shared with me part of his journey back to faith. He had received the news that his mother had cancer, and he was returning from the West Coast to be with her. As the day grew late, he pulled over to the side of the road to sleep, and when morning came, he was a witness to one of the most beautiful sunrises he had ever seen—a panoramic view of the skyline above the flat rocks surrounding him. It was a message to him, at this place, at this time of God's all-encompassing love for him—and for his family. His eyes brightened as he shared this story with me. He had turned to face his Father in heaven, and that same Father had "run" to be with him, sharing the miracle of sunrise with him. He knew that this was for him. God found him, and he was changed.

How is God trying to get your attention? Are you in a strange land? Have you come to your senses? After you experience God's love, it won't be difficult to love back; it won't be as difficult to love others either. You will see things you have never seen before and hear things you have never heard. You will be in a "forever" relationship, not temporary foster care, and you will not find it hard to follow God around, just as Sidney still seeks to be close to me.

I stood there praying and then blessing those who had tuned in to the service. As I had been sharing the homily, two young women had walked in and sat down in chairs along the side of the chapel. It was a strange experience speaking to two "visible" people and who knows how many "invisible" patients. As I made eye contact with the two women, I noticed that they were both crying. Dog stories can do that to you. Especially when God uses them to embody His grace...

God on Both Sides of the Equation

Whenever I am with patients, I am always listening for commonality. This forms a bridge between us that is easier to cross into the more serious matters. It doesn't always lead to spiritual or emotional depth but certainly can. Commonality also supports bonding, as does the use of "we" instead of "I" when appropriate. It is a gentle way in and builds rapport.

One danger of commonality is that I can so easily fall into my own storytelling, which takes the focus off of the patient and puts it on me. I have to always remember to keep my sharing in check so that my vision and hearing are not clouded with my own experiences. Minimal self-disclosure!

I love it when patients bring up the subject of dogs! I believe dogs are a gift to us and show so many of the characteristics of God—almost as if God put His fingerprint on them. They are also a real and beneficial example of listening. Not only is their sense of listening acute, but they also read the non-verbal cues better than most human beings. They know when to come alongside, and they seem to understand tears. They also meet our deep need for unconditional love.

Listening with openness and compassion might eventually open us up to share when it is our turn to do so, usually in a different venue. My homily is one example of how God has used my listening to speak up about other important things.

When I listen, I am also attuned to "parallel" feelings and take note of these. When Mrs. J shared that she felt bad about her dog being "shuffled around," she was experiencing the same feelings. I didn't bring this up to her, but realizing it helped me better understand her feelings.

Listening with the Heart

- Think of a lesson you learned that has stuck with you. How can you use this to help others? If you have already done this, what happened as a result of your sharing your lesson?
- When you hear that you have something in common with the person you care about, do you feel the freedom to share? How do you keep from turning the focus on to yourself?
- How can you become more like a "dog" to others?
- We love because we are first loved. Many people will experience God but not call it God. They may have an experience that brings them to their knees, something so profound that it is beyond words. Are you able to join them in their joy and gratitude?

CHAPTER 8
GOD OF THE UNEXPECTED

> *He fished in his pocket for his keys and instead pulled out the last geode, gray and smooth, earth-shaped. He held it, warming in his palm, thinking of all mysteries the world contained: layers of stone, concealed beneath the flesh of earth and grass; these dull rocks, with their glimmering hidden hearts.*
>
> —Kim Edwards, *The Memory Keeper's Daughter*

There is a geode on my desk. It has been cut in half and polished on its flat side. Turned to the wall, it is grey, nondescript and rather ugly. Turned with its cut side toward me, I view layers of luminosity in differing shades of blue, crackled and splayed out like rays of a star. The irregular center is outlined in a deeper blue, and within, it is cushioned in crystals, its intricate patterns not fully visible to the naked eye. The symmetry inside is comforting and predictable but not without mystery. I may see the "what" and may only barely comprehend the "how," but the "why" eludes me.

Several years ago, I had the opportunity to visit with adult hospice patients in a downtown hospital. I usually worked with children, but I was being trained on a new PDA (tablet) for record keeping, and Father Brown, the hospice chaplain who was stationed at the hospital, was one of the trainers. So, I accompanied him on his rounds to learn the process of using, recording, and downloading patient information into the main computer program from the PDA.

We visited Mr. O on this particular morning on the oncology wing. Mr. O had lung cancer and was admitted to hospice when he was admitted to the hospital the day before. To most people, I learned, being admitted to hospice is a death sentence. No one stops to think that he or she will be dying anyway or that death is already imminent. When a person comes to hospice, the word that stands out is *death*, not Comfort Care. And then, when the chaplain comes in, the person may feel that they are face-to-face with *death* itself. What a welcome!

Mr. O, on the other hand, seemed genuinely glad to see us. Father Brown talked pleasantries with him and then asked him a pointed question.

"How are you and God doing, Mr. O?" Mr. O almost smiled. He was a bit difficult to understand, as he was heavy with illness, but I did hear, "Praise Jesus!" and "Everything is good!"

We talked with him for a few more minutes. As we were readying ourselves to leave, Father Brown touched Mr. O's head and blessed him. He then took his hand and told him that we would see him later.

I reached over to take Mr. O's hand ready to say good-bye. It was then that he grabbed my hand and held on to it very tightly. And then he began to pray in tongues, which to many chaplains might have been alarming, but fortunately, I had experienced this before. I wished I could have understood his words because they may have been a comfort to me, and I was certainly in need of comfort.

It had been an exceptionally difficult week. On Monday morning, I had attended a special session on "Occurrences," the handling of mistakes, incidents, theft, etc. and how to report them. I did not normally come in on Mondays, but my boss had requested that I attend since I was a rather new employee. While I was in the meeting in our own conference room, my wallet was taken out of my purse and disappeared into who-knows-where. When I discovered the loss, I thought it was a well-planned joke meant to frighten us into locking up our purses. I had left mine on the floor in my office, wide open, as an invitation to anyone who had peeked into my cubicle. Someone, apparently, had accepted the invitation and taken my wallet, heavily laden with credit cards, checks, driver's license, social security card, receipts, a myriad of other cards, and sixteen lousy dollars.

I immediately called home and asked my sons to check everywhere around the house they could think of... no luck. I walked to my car and looked under the seats, in the trunk and between the seats... no luck. I went back into my office and looked under my desk, in my cubby, in my office trash can, and everywhere I could think of... no luck. I was truly a victim of theft. Unbelievable!

I rose to the occasion, had my boss report the theft for me, went home to search one last time and began the long process of reporting everything I could remember, going to the bank to close out accounts and open new ones. I even went immediately to the Secretary of State's office to apply for a new driver's license. I was not yet done with everything on my list, but I needed to take a break from the whole incident. I thought I was doing quite well, as I usually do in a crisis, but then I began to fall apart a few days later, wondering why in the world I was crying and upset.

These episodes are usually one thing masked as another and can be confusing. They begin with my feeling all alone. All of the negative things that have happened to me in the past few days begin to form themselves into a little inventory list with notes attached: *No one will ever really want you. Your husband is too busy to care about you. You're a lousy mother. Your kids are a mess.* Instead of crying for the world, its darkness, sadness, and brokenness (which is why I was *really* crying), the tears came packaged in self-recrimination and bad feelings about who I was and what I was about—ministering to hospice patients.

I should have seen this coming. Think about it. I finally land a job that is my heart's desire. I get to pray on the job and talk about spiritual things all day long if I like. I get to hear all kinds of stories—the sublime, the challenging, the inspiring. And then my wallet is stolen.

The following day my manager, during our team meeting, asked me to call Steven's mother, Terry. Terry did not like female "pastors." But Terry was in crisis—her son, Steven was dying, and my boss thought she would be open to my coming. While I was driving the forty miles to the visit, I envisioned taking her for a walk, praying with her, hugging her, comforting her.

Instead, when I called her from my car, she told me she was fine, that her pastor had been out to see her, that she knew that I *had* to come anyway, but she was really OK. She didn't need my visit. I was so naive!

At first, I thought, *Well, your loss... God wants to bless you through me, and you have just shut God down.* Later that day, the message turned into, *You really aren't needed. What are you doing in this business anyway?*

I took Wednesday off. I went for a walk, loved up my dog and helped my son out by giving his dogs a bath. He had moved in down the street from us and had demolished much of his home to ready it for refurbishing. It needed new plumbing, electricity, and a second bathroom, among other things. The puppies had been christened by the dust and filth, and it was my job to clean them up. They were so well-behaved. I began to feel a little better. I spent some time meditating and cruised through a spiritual direction session with Charlene, one of my directees. She was such a joy to be with, to guide through her spiritual walk with God. Ironically, she had been feeling unappreciated by people but very much appreciated by God. I was in the throes of the same thing but was clueless at the time.

Thursday came. Sherry, the children's hospice nurse, and Cathy, the social worker, and I drove over to a local athletic company store to purchase a little outfit for James who was going to Children's Hospital for the weekend on respite so that his mother could get some down time. (Hospice provides this for the caregivers of those in hospice.) We wanted to send him home in style when he was discharged. On the way back from the store, Sherry made some noises about being depressed. When we got back to the office, she asked Cathy if she could spend some time with her.

There I was, a degree in counseling, years of living experiences, sitting in my office alone with my paperwork and computer while Cathy had a "session" with Sherry. This voice in my head said, *You didn't want to get mixed up in that whole mess anyway, did you?* Sherry was very high strung and had a suitcase full of issues. My head was logical, but my heart cried out, *Doesn't anyone want* my *skill set?* which was a crazy response since I had just enjoyed a session with Charlene the night before, and she had asked for *more* of my business cards.

To top off the day, Sherry, Cathy, and I went over to see Jonah. He was another hospice baby. We were on the way to his house to meet his mother for the second time, and she called five minutes before the meeting to say that she had taken Jonah to his grandmother's house. Could we please drive over there to visit him? Grandma lived on the west side of town, and we were parked on Jonah's street on the east side. Sherry said no to Jonah's mother, and that was that. We all drove home from there. Lucky for Cathy and me, we were only about a mile from home. Not so lucky for Sherry. She had to drive more than thirty miles in rush hour traffic.

The first time we visited Jonah's home, we stood at the door peering in at Jonah's aunt as his mother called and told us she had to work overtime and couldn't make it. Could we please reschedule? It wasn't as if we could fire Jonah's mother. We only had five pediatric patients at the time. But that's another story...

When I got home that Thursday night, I was beat. I mean, I could hardly put one foot in front of the other. I made a freezer-to-table dinner for myself and my two sons. While we were eating, my youngest made some comment about no one being willing to help him clean up his house... no one. He had asked around. No one had any time. I had just told him I was so tired I couldn't possibly come over and help. Well, you know what happened. There I was sweating and sneezing and helping. I did limit it to one hour—some kind of boundary kicked in—and came home and fell into bed at 8:30 p.m.

My husband was taking a final for a class, and I expected him to pop in bed beside me around 10:00 p.m. so that I could at least get a hug or two. Instead, I woke up at 11:15 p.m. searching the house for him. I saw his shoes, so I knew he was home. He came walking in from the studio office behind the garage as my oldest son came through the door. The two of them had stayed up late talking. I sleepily said, "I need you," to my husband and went back to bed. But by the time he came to bed, I was blubbering, sniffing, and dropping tears all over myself. I didn't have any words left to speak as I turned over and fell asleep.

First thing the next morning, I did get a hug, but I still didn't feel much like talking. I went on to work, took the shuttle to the hospital, and spent the morning with Father Brown. I yawned my way through the morning but did happen to semi-pray over Mr. B who was actively dying, met Ms. R in the hallway as she was sloppily dressed to go to the hospice residence that day, and sat by Mr. O's bedside as he delivered a message from God to me via his cancer-ridden body.

My eyes telescoped in reverse to the geode. The memory of Mr. O's uninterpretable message to me has stayed with me for these past several years. Here was a man, very slight, very sick, and very simple. His outer shell was ignoble, greyed, nondescript, and rather ugly. He was poor and uneducated, more dependent on others than ever as he lived out the last few days of his life. But he had a message for me—not Father Brown, but me. What was it? I may never know for sure, but I do know that it had an electric effect on me. Somehow, I knew that I was loved and cared for, that the work I was doing was worth something, that *I* was worth something. In spite of the previous week's discouragement, I was given encouragement to continue on the path I had begun.

There was something about Mr. O. Though he was nothing much to look at on the outside, there was something within him that sparkled, a mystery of sorts, that he knew he had to share with me. I'll treasure those few moments for a lifetime.

God on Both Sides of the Equation

Some days I feel as if I receive so much more than I give. This story reflects that truth. I had so much going on inside of me that I felt pretty useless to my patients. It wasn't that I didn't care. I was depleted, and I had not taken the time to debrief with anyone. This was also before I started my Clinical Pastoral Education, and I was not aware that trauma and endless giving could be devastating in my attempts to care for others. Self-care is vital for ourselves and for those we serve.

One of the red flags of burnout is that everything becomes all about me. I begin to turn inward. Unfortunately, I was unable to see this when I was experiencing it. It was only later that I realized what was taking place.

Normally, I would have interpreted the mother who resisted my visit as a person who needed to be in control of something since she had no control over her son's demise.

I truly believe that God understood what was happening and that God intervened through an encounter that was, in the end, more for me than for the patient. Of course, I prayed sincerely for him, but when I was finished, God was *not* finished. I finally began to listen. God had my attention, and even though I did not understand what was being said to me, I knew in my spirit that it was for me. This man was intent on giving me a gift from God even as he neared death. What a selfless act of grace.

Which brings me to something that we, as people of faith, take for granted yet sometimes ignore. Are you listening for God in your daily journey? Not just Scriptures and not just sermons. Are you noticing the work of God as it happens? I can so often lose the significance of something if I am not listening to God's still, small voice. God ministers to us through others—sometimes the most unlikely of people. God is the God of the unexpected. Just when you think you understand how things work, God turns them upside down. So creative!

Listening to Your Heart

- When do you think was the last time God was trying to get your attention? Were you listening and did you change your behavior because of it?
- Can you think of times when you really needed to take a break but just kept on moving? How did things turn out? How do you think God ministered to you during that time?
- When discouragement piles up, how do you regain your sense of who you really are?
- Are you able to recognize when something is wrong inside of you? What steps did you take to further understand what was happening?
- Is there a difference between selfishness and self-care? Are you aware that a lack of self-care can lead to selfishness and make you more self-centered?

CHAPTER 9
LET GOD BE THE JUDGE

I am the one who has seen affliction
by the rod of his wrath.
He has driven me away and made me
walk
in darkness rather than light;
indeed, he has turned his hand against
me
again and again, all day long.

—Lamentations 3:1

Late one early summer evening while I was on call at the hospital, the Emergency Center alerted me that I was needed in Trauma to support a Level 2 patient (serious but not deadly). A new intern, Robert, who was shadowing me this shift, accompanied me through the swinging doors to the trauma area. The team—doctors, nurses, a patient representative, a respiratory therapist, an x-ray technician, a phlebotomist, among others—gathered around the patient on the third gurney and performed their predetermined tasks. A hit and run driver had ploughed into a twenty-year-old female pedestrian. While she was in considerable pain, her injuries were not life threatening. She was treated and moved into Area A of the Emergency Center. I had observed her treatment from the sidelines, watching and waiting for family and checking in with the patient representative for updates on her condition.

After she had been wheeled out of the Trauma Center, I approached her as she lay in the hallway waiting for an empty curtained cubicle. My eyes met hers.

"Are you OK?" I checked in.

"Yeah, but angry that someone could do this to me and then just take off. Do you think they'll find the person who did this to me?"

"I know they'll try. Your family's been contacted. Would you like me to stay with you until they arrive?"

"No, thanks, I'm really OK."

Easy. A little questioning. Some frustration. But reasonably OK. Manageable. It was already after midnight, and I expected things to settle down. I was looking forward to going up to the sleep room in an hour or two and resting a bit.

Robert and I returned to the office area to run a new list of patients so we could resume visits in the Emergency Center with something to hold on to as we approached the next cycle of patients. My pager went off. Robert and I stared at each other. "So much for a quiet night!" he laughed as he straightened up his askew lab coat and ran a hand through his hair. Robert was a harpist. I envied him as he wheeled his magical instrument through the corridors of the hospital on his visits to patients. He had an easy "in." Patients, visitors and nurses alike were drawn to him like fruit flies to apples. I had no such talent and had to initiate every first word on my visits. Life was *so* unfair!

I picked up the phone and dialed the emergency area.

Gavin answered. "We have a Level I Trauma on its way to us. Please come down here as soon as possible. This one's going to be tough. Another hit and run pedestrian accident." He quickly hung up.

We left the office and hurried on to the elevator. It was late and neither one of us was feeling much like chatting. The ride down and walk over was quiet and a bit ominous.

We entered the Trauma room from the family side, scooting aside as a middle-aged man was brought in, an EMT rhythmically pushing on his chest as they wheeled him into the center area of the trauma room.

We then stood off to the side, asking if any family had accompanied him. He had been transferred from a sister hospital after being hit by a car while walking through a trailer park. The driver had left the scene. The family had not yet been notified, and so we decided to wait for a few minutes. While we were standing in the background, the doctor in charge asked for a stool and then requested that everyone stand back. The patient had no pulse. I had no idea what he had in mind until I heard him crack open the patient's chest and then watched as he pulled out his heart and began massaging it. A pharmacist came over and administered two shots into the heart. They detected a very weak pulse then wheeled the patient off to an operating room. Robert and I had witnessed this but had not fully absorbed what we had seen. We were more concerned about the family finding out about their loved one.

After we had visited twenty more patients in the Emergency area, Robert left for home at 2:00 a.m., and I went up to the sleeping room. At 3:30 a.m., I received a call from the 5th floor Intensive Care Unit. The patient pedestrian who had been brought into Trauma had expired, and the family was now with him. The nurse requested that I come up to be with the family.

I entered the room and quietly introduced myself. Before I made my way to his wife, I noticed that the patient was still bloodied and dirty. He had not been cleaned up as I had expected. I excused myself for a moment and connected with the attending nurse.

"Why hasn't the patient been cleaned up?" I gently inquired.

"Oh, because this is a hit-and-run, a *crime,* we can't touch his injuries until the police have come and assessed the situation." I know she was doing what she had learned, but somehow it seemed so incredibly insensitive to allow the family to see him in this condition.

I reentered the room and spent extended time with each family member present moving deftly from one to another. Grief displayed itself in a myriad of ways. His wife was solemn, tearless and vigilant. His sister wept non-stop, praying that God would bring her brother back to life, caressing his chest and face. His brother-in-law wrapped his arm around his wife. His niece began to sob noisily and collapsed at the foot of the bed. I brought a chair over to her and put my arm around her for a few moments. I asked the family if they wanted me to pray.

His sister mouthed, "Yes," as the rest of the family nodded. We held hands and prayed.

After spending some time with the immediate family, I went out into the hall to see if any extended family was present. His parents were there and noiselessly and hesitantly crept into the room. They appeared to be in shock. There were no tears, but when the bereavement representative came in, there were non-stop questions from his father—his way of dealing with the pain... perhaps more information would help.

After the bereavement rep left, I asked the family if they would like to sing *Amazing Grace*.

"That was one of my son's favorite sacred songs," his mother whispered. We all held hands and sang, and then the sister abruptly took me aside.

"My brother wasn't saved. Actually, he was pretty antagonistic about our faith. Dan and I are missionaries to inner city St. Louis.

Harvey used to tease us about our work. Like he disdained us for it." She wept shamelessly, shaking her head back and forth. I took her by the shoulders and looked her in the eyes.

"You know, God is just, merciful, *and* loving. Why don't we allow God to decide the outcome here?" Maybe I was being a bit insensitive to her concerns, but she nodded to me and turned to caress Harvey once again. One thing I have had ingrained into me time and time again—Don't prejudge *any* situation. Who am I to presume the mind of God? Let God be the judge!

"Is there anything else I can do to help out?"

"No, thanks, Chaplain," Dad replied, looking as if he was processing what lay before him, unsure of the reality of what he was seeing.

"I'll leave you alone with Harvey now and let you say good-bye. Please let me know if you need anything else. You can have the nurse page me."

"We'll do that," Dad replied, as if this was a matter of procedure and protocol.

I walked out of the Intensive Care Unit and made my way down to the office. It was 5:00 a.m., and I decided to stay up and read for an hour until the shift was over.

I left at 6:00 a.m., went out to breakfast with my husband, and went to bed the moment I got home. All seemed to be well.

The following afternoon as I awoke, I detected a deep sadness rising within me. I wasn't quite sure at the time what to attribute it to. Perhaps I hadn't gotten quite enough sleep. Perhaps it was the added responsibility of taking care of our son's three birds, two dogs, and two fish on top of our own three dogs while he was on vacation. Maybe it was the fact that my husband's parents had just left after spending a few hours with us. They were in the process of deciding whether or not to move back to Michigan from Illinois. Maybe it was because Father's Day was approaching, and I missed my father who died in 1994 of a massive heart attack at the age of seventy-six.

I took all of these things into account, continued to feel a sense of loss, buried it and proceeded to get ready for a BBQ at a friend's house. However, on the way to the party, I felt tears welling up in my eyes, and a feeling that I might become physically ill. It was then, as the anger started to surface, that I realized I was reacting primarily to what I had seen and experienced the night before. I was having a delayed reaction.

How could someone hit a living human being and leave the scene? (And this had happened twice in one night!) What was happening within the person who ran into the patient? This person is also a child of God. How will they live with themselves knowing what they had done to this family? Why did the doctor have to perform such a violent act in the trauma room? Did it really have a chance of succeeding or was he being overly dramatic? Why wasn't the patient brought directly to this hospital instead of our sister hospital where time was lost that might have made a difference? Why was he killed the night before his son's high school graduation party? He had been walking to the store to pick up a few more items for the party when he had been hit. It was raining and dark. Why didn't he take his car instead? Why does the family now have to have a funeral instead of a party? All of the out-of-town guests thought they were coming to celebrate. Now they will be mourning! How will the person who hit him ever forgive themselves? Why do I (and others) feel the need to assign blame?

My concept of suffering is changing. I see the inherent darkness in the world much more clearly. When we do not value human life, a reckless act becomes something to respond to nonchalantly. When violence is portrayed on television night after night, we don't recognize the real thing when it happens. It's as if we're numb. We are absolutely broken when we disconnect from good character, morals, and timeless truths. When we as a people decide to run our own lives, control our own destinies, and take things into our own hands, we make a royal mess of everything! We so often forget that every single person is a child of God, and that given the right circumstances, we, too, take part in the hurt and violence in the world.

A friend of mine has been sharing his reading with me of the *Epistle to the Romans* by Karl Barth. Barth asserts that all evil and suffering gives us an opportunity to seek comfort and help from our Creator, that it may even act as a magnet to draw people to God, giving Him an opening into their lives. It's almost as if a door gently opens in the middle of the crisis. Will we see it? Will we walk through it?

C.S. Lewis states in *The Problem of Pain*, "...pain insists upon being attended to. God whispers to us in our pleasures, speaks in our conscience, but shouts in our pains: it is his megaphone to rouse a deaf world...(it) is a terrible instrument; it may lead to final and unrepentant rebellion. But it gives the only opportunity (one) can have for amendment. It removes the veil; it plants the flag of truth within the fortress of a rebel soul."

St. Augustine has said, "God wants to give us something, but cannot because our hands are full—there's nowhere for Him to put it." Suffering opens up a space in our lives to give God an opportunity to draw us to Himself, especially when we experience empty hands.

Lewis further shares, "When I think of pain—of anxiety that gnaws like fire and loneliness that spreads out like a desert, and the heartbreaking routine of monotonous misery, or again of dull aches that blacken our whole landscape or sudden nauseating pains that knock a man's heart out at one blow, of pains that seem already intolerable and then are suddenly increased, of infuriating scorpion-stinging pains that startle into maniacal movement a man who seemed half dead with his previous tortures—it 'quite overcrowds my spirit.' If I knew any way of escape I would crawl through sewers to find it. But what is the good of telling you about my feelings? You know them already: they are the same as yours. I am not arguing that pain is not painful. Pain hurts. That is what the word means. I am only trying to show that the old Christian doctrine of being made 'perfect through suffering' (Hebrews 2:10) is not incredible."

He goes on to say that the tribulations we experience cannot cease until God sees us remade. Does this mean that God has a hand in our suffering? I would hope that is not true, but I cannot say for sure. I only know that each time I have been in pain, it caused me to run into His arms. And I also recall the scripture that says, "He who did not spare his own Son, but gave him up for us all—how will he not also, along with him, graciously give us all things?" (Rom. 8.32). Our suffering can end as Jesus' did—it can give us back our true selves, resurrected and pure.

As I sit and reflect upon what I have written, I wonder if I have intellectualized suffering. I think not. I have seen it up close, and it is ugly. It takes many forms and many faces. As I sit and examine that same precious geode that sits on my desk, I am reminded of Harvey's father. A hard case covers the preciousness inside. It is dull, nondescript, and easily overlooked. The danger in viewing and entering into suffering with others is the risk of hardening, of taking the experience, the witness, and leaving it locked inside the casing. It takes an enormous vulnerability to allow the casing to be chiseled away in order to see and experience the beauty inside or expose the hurt.

So, can I see any benefit for the family who has lost their father or their son in such a brutal manner? What about the person who hit the patient? Perhaps these circumstances will serve to give God an opening to fill the empty space in their lives that only He can fill. It may cause the opposite reaction—they may run from God in anger and hatred or self-loathing. It is a risk it seems God is willing to take to have us back in communion with Himself. It has certainly given me much to think and pray about.

God on Both Sides of the Equation

"Hit and run" leaves so many unanswered questions. "Why?" is usually the first question one asks when something terrible happens. Then, I usually ask, "How? How can God use this for my good?"

"Hit and run" does not have to be related to an automobile accident. It can be *any* event that causes us interminable pain. I recall a time in my life when I was in so much pain, which transformed itself into depression, that I could not even pray. And I was unable to listen to God, hear God. I felt grossly empty and numbed from the inside out. It took ten years and God making Himself known in a very creative way to break the shell over my heart and allow me to hear again and then, to listen.

Watching and listening to each person in the patient's room was critical for my ministering to each one of them. They each reacted differently, and so, I had to care for each one uniquely. While it might have been tempting to treat them all alike and be done with it, I know I would not have been truly listening if I had done that. As humans, too, it is tempting to find one way to relate to pain in others and then simply apply it when necessary. My guess, however, is that the one hurting can sense the insincerity in this. Trust certainly would be eroded.

Taking the time to listen and then gauge your response accordingly is vital to being fully present to the other. One size never fits all.

My delayed reaction to this trauma was not conscious. I had to set aside my own grief and allow the pain of those around me to take precedence. I believe it comes from practice and from the work of God within me. At some point, it is important to realize that these situations are not about *me,* at least not in the moment. As I experienced the pain on the way to the BBQ, I was eventually aware of what it was, and I allowed it to wash over me. Grief can be delayed but never fully avoided.

Listening to Your Heart

- How do you feel when the person you are caring for isn't "cleaned up?" Are you distracted by the raw pain of what is presented to you? What might be a helpful way to respond to this? Are you able to see the person beyond what is presented to you?
- How do you know when grace is appropriate and when it might be helpful to be direct and honest? How might you be in danger of using directness as a club, trying to put forth your own agenda?
- Have you ever had a delayed reaction to suffering or trauma? When the pain finally seeped out, were you able to administer self-care or seek out the care of another person?
- Do you ever expect that people will experience grief similarly? How could listening guide you?
- Have you ever been the cause of someone else's pain and grief? What happens to your judgement when you are the one who brings sorrow to others?
- When you have caused harm to someone else, how do you deal with your suffering?

CHAPTER 10
A TINY WINDOW OF OPPORTUNITY

Little is much when God is in it!...
In the mad rush of the broad way,
In the hurry and the strife,
Tell of Jesus' love and mercy,
Give to them the Word of Life.

—*Kittie Louise Suffield (1884-1972)*

Today is September 29, 2010. Summer seems like a shadow now, as if it really didn't happen at all. Or if it did, it was for a moment, and then it was gone.

I always pick up the free monthly gardening magazine at the local nursery when I'm there. As I leafed through it, my fingers swiftly moved to the page where it tells me what is due for the month. Time to plant grass seed; time to plant shrubs and trees; time to move the houseplants indoors; time to allow the roses to form rosehips, which is a signal to the roses that fall is coming, and they can prepare to go dormant; time to divide the perennials.

Under each heading are detailed instructions and a list of tasks for the month. September seems to be busier than most months except, perhaps, for spring. Much preparation is needed for the cold, barren months ahead. Protection is crucial, as well as making sure feeding has taken place to sustain life in the plant as it travels through dormancy.

But there is such a small window of time for this preparation. Soon, autumn will feel as fleeting as summer. The *Farmers' Almanac* has predicted snow for Thanksgiving this year.

I've begun to depend on *Michigan Gardener: Your Guide to Great Lakes Gardening* for my monthly to-do lists. A couple of weeks ago, the September issue had not yet been delivered to my favorite nursery and, truth be told, I really hadn't had time to deal with the outside tasks. My sister had come up from Tennessee to help me sort through more of Mom's and Dad's stuff, mostly family pictures—a very time-consuming task. I had spent a few days on a mini vacation with my husband, and now I was paying for all of this with a backlog of tasks with yard work at the top of the list.

I picked up the magazine two days ago, and now I have exactly two days to complete the task list before the October list is printed and distributed—impossible! Such a tiny window! Not to mention that today is the first non-rainy day we've had for a while. I always thought I was rather good at prioritizing, but today I feel a bit overwhelmed. At least I can plant the bulbs and rhizomes I purchased last week, if nothing else. If I don't get them in before winter, I won't have the display I desire in the spring, and who knows, the bulbs might even rot while waiting for me! And then, there's the grass seed—dated for 2010. So, that *has* to go in. OK, I think I can do this. If there's time left over, I can add a few more things… maybe divide those perennials!

Sometimes I feel overwhelmed in a similar way when I encounter a patient in the hospital who has a myriad of problems—physical, social, psychological, and spiritual. Under the circumstances, and considering the commitment we have to "visit every patient every day," I'm fortunate to have five to ten minutes per patient. Not only that, but because my clinical days are not back to back, I seldom see each patient a second time. Many are discharged before I return, and so, I have a tiny window of opportunity to minister to the person in the bed.

This was the scenario when I was called down to the Observation area to visit Mr. J, an Black man who happened to be a few years younger than myself. The nurse in Observation, a subunit of the Emergency Center, had called the Spiritual Care office, and they had paged me. Mr. J had asked for me specifically, and I was mystified as to why until I entered his cubicle to listen and speak with him.

I came down to the Emergency Center as quickly as I could. I was due to be signed out for the day, but when a patient request comes in, I see it as priority. I suppose I could have passed the request on to the incoming chaplain, but knowing that this man had asked specifically for me, I wanted to handle it personally.

I knocked softly on the wall next to Mr. J's curtained cubicle.

"Come in, Chaplain, I've been waiting for you."

The nurse poked her head in and said, "We're getting ready to discharge Mr. J shortly." Which, in "nursalese" means, "Please try to make it short since we have to free up the space for another patient."

I turned to find a place to sit, an institutional chair near the foot of his bed.

"Before we begin, Chaplain, I want to tell you something and then ask you a few questions," he initiated.

"That would be fine," I responded.

"Well, I want to tell you why I asked for you. You see, you prayed with my wife when she was on 9 South a few months ago. I so appreciated your prayer, I just knew you were the right one to talk to," he smiled and winced at the same time.

"I feel honored that you asked for me, Mr. J."

"Well, now I need to ask you a few questions... Are you a 'born-again' believer? Do you, Chaplain Johnson, believe in the Holy Spirit?"

Inside, I was asserting, *You have no idea how much I believe in the Holy Spirit. In fact, that's why I'm even here in this hospital. It was He who orchestrated all of this for me!* Verbally, I said, "Yes and yes, Mr. J."

"OK, then." Once that was settled, his story began to slowly unfold before me like a precious but fragile manuscript that had been folded and unfolded many times but never fully shared with another soul. I knew I was in a very sacred space.

"My life seems like such a waste. I've been given so many chances, and I've blown every one of them. It started with small, insignificant crimes, nothing that really mattered or bothered anyone too much. And then it grew into the tough stuff." He looked down at the floor. I watched sadness filter through his entire body leaving him limp and almost lifeless.

"Tell me about your conversion," I encouraged. I knew that we would have to draw on this later on in the conversation, so I wanted him to plant the seeds now. The Holy Spirit is so good at watering those seeds.

"Well, my mother died when I was thirteen. As I said, I was already into the tough stuff by then. I ended up in a detention facility in Tennessee. I became a Christian while I was incarcerated. There was this woman who came to the prison to share Jesus with us on a regular basis. She gave an invitation—whoever wanted to ask Jesus into his life was to come up and pray with her. So, I did. I even have her picture here."

He stopped, pulled out his cell phone, pushed a few buttons and scrolled to a colorful picture. "Here she is, Missus Ott."

I pulled in closer and took the cell phone out of his hand. He was a little younger when the picture was taken and was standing by a slight, light-haired woman. Her silver hair was swept up on her head, and she was dressed plainly but elegantly. Both of them were grinning into the camera, arms wrapped around one another.

"We still keep in touch. You see, after I was released from detention, she had me over for dinner at her house. She even invited me to go to church with her. There was a lot of slander about that. A lot of the people at the church were racist. They didn't care much for me being in their service, but she didn't care. She loved me... but..." Tears came to his eyes.

"I lied to her. She defended me after I was accused of a crime. I was guilty, but I told her I didn't do it, and she stuck up for me. She even called in her high-powered attorney, and I was off the hook. She vouched for me, and I let her down."

"Can you tell her the truth?" I urged.

"No, I can't. She'd be *so* disappointed in me. I just can't."

I felt saddened by his response. I had hoped that he could experience the freedom in truthfulness, even if it was painful.

"You know, Mr. J, we're all broken people." I took him by the hand and looked into his eyes. "I'm just as broken in God's sight as you are. God works best with those who are broken."

He shook his head, as if that was an impossible idea. "I'm still in thick with the wrong people."

"It's never too late. How can you best honor Mrs. Ott? Is there someone you can pass hope on to as she passed it on to you?"

"I don't know. All I can do these days is sit in my chair in the house. My arthritis is so bad, I can hardly move."

"Loving someone else doesn't take much movement. Is there someone you can love and give the attention to that you received when you were so needy?" I prodded.

"You don't understand. If I change, even in the least little bit, my life is over. They'll be out for me. I'll be a dead man." He looked up at me, his eyes widening.

I wondered what he was involved in. I didn't need to know, but I sat there realizing that we were two people sitting face-to-face, holding hands and sharing our hearts with one another. For the moments given to us, we occupied the same space.

"How does your faith address your fear? I think of Jesus. He chose to do what was right, knowing that he would put himself in danger." I looked at him unblinkingly.

He nodded. He understood.

The nurse poked her head around the curtain. "We have to sign out Mr. J now."

I looked at him. He looked at me. "Can I pray with you before I go?"

"Yes, Chaplain."

I prayed, heart-broken at the life he had shared with me. I knew that he had some very difficult decisions to make in the future. At the same time, I knew that nothing was irredeemable. No one with an open heart is ever turned away from God.

Our time together was so short, really only a few minutes. How could I address his needs in such a short time? The opportunity was so very small, and the needs were enormous. It was at the end of the day, the end of my shift. His bed was being made available for another patient. There were limits, severe limits.

So, today, when I close my computer and silently say another prayer for Mr. J, I go out to plant bulbs and grass seed and divide my perennials. According to the task list in the magazine, I only have two days to do this before another list is published, adding to my commitments to the yard. Such a small window of opportunity!

Yet, I do know that if I take just a few minutes to plant the bulbs and the seed, I will be rewarded amply in the spring. If I take the time—just a few minutes—to divide the perennials, someone else will have a chance to enjoy the beauty of the flowers in their yard next summer, and my perennials will have more freedom to grow with a little more space, unencumbered by the additional leaves and roots of their neighbors. I can do this hopefully because I know that I am only responsible for putting the bulbs into the ground, scattering the seeds, and pulling up and dividing the perennials. I must trust God for the results.

God on Both Sides of the Equation

Caring and listening do not have to be a long process. If my spirit is uncluttered (and even if it isn't, God can clear the clutter away!), I can allow life to pour through me to another.

In my case, a relationship had already been somewhat developed—all in less than five minutes—through a prayer prayed over Mrs. J months before. God had planted something in Mr. J that invisibly connected to something in me. It was revived at just the right time.

At times, I have spent well over an hour with one person when it was needed. That's not always possible. So, I take what I can and allow God to do the inside work in His own time.

Whenever I can and whenever it seems appropriate, I try to draw on the person of Jesus with those who are Christian. I believe Jesus identified with everything we humans deal with while He was on earth—except maybe the challenge of aging! Imagine the emotions, thoughts, and actions that coursed through him as a human being—regret, sadness, joy, loss, disappointment, anger, abandonment, taking life-threatening risks, giving grace to those who did not deserve it, taking time to listen, knowing Himself and knowing God, always having the care of others at the forefront. He did initiate self-care when it was needed and spent time with His Father to replenish His soul.

Scripture is full of events, parables, and stories that, when applied appropriately in a caring relationship, can place a comforting buffer around a person or can present a decision made in faith when it is time to make a decision. Mr. J used this time to "work out his own salvation" by sharing his story with me, releasing some of the shame he has carried.

I am so thankful that I grew up in a denomination that valued Scripture and its memorization. Not every chaplain has been graced with this gift. While we minister to all people and bring each person's faith tradition to the surface to provide strength and comfort, I am always grateful for the opportunity to draw on my own tradition.

Listening to Your Heart

- How do you feel and respond when someone you are caring for shares a secret with you that could be risky? (This does not fall under the category of having to report anything to the authorities regarding self-harm or possible homicide.) How do you know if you should try to talk them out of something or simply give them a different perspective?
- It usually helps to have a person share his/her story with you. Why do you think it is important to listen to a person's story? What might be the motivation for telling his/her story to you?
- On the opposite side of a listening relationship, how do you know when it is time to "wrap things up," especially when there are no time limits involved? How can you gracefully leave a person who loves to talk?

CHAPTER 11
AN ANGEL'S TOUCH

"'To touch can be to give life,' said Michelangelo, and he was absolutely right."

—*Dacher Keltner*

The room was darkened, smudged by the twilight attempting to sneak through the closed hospital curtains. David was my last visit of the day before I began my long drive home, weaving my way through freeway traffic like a needle through stubborn fabric. To say I was tired would be a shocking understatement. In the past three days, I had worked an overnight, attended class, and was now wrapping up my long clinical day on the floor.

Before I entered David's room, I muttered a prayer and glanced within to see a woman on her cell phone with her back to the door. A younger man sat on a wheeled stool across from the foot of the bed, up against the wall. Their son, I presumed. The sound of oxygen being administered was punctuating the space, ironically sounding like life but given to soften the blows of death.

I spoke to the son briefly and introduced myself as the chaplain rounding on this floor. He silently nodded, afraid to speak or exhausted and uninvested due to lack of sleep.

As soon as Mrs. C flipped her cell phone shut, she turned around. I walked over to her with an outstretched hand. "Hi. My name is Pat, one of the chaplains. I'm rounding on this floor today."

"Nice to meet you. I'm Jennie."

"How is your husband doing today?"

"Do you know his history?"

"No, I don't."

"He's been very ill for about six years. We're all surprised that he's lived this long. He was in the hospital for five days and then discharged to hospice, but he needed a particular kind of oxygen, and he had to come back..." She looked me in the eyes. "David doesn't talk much about his faith. I really wish he would. Sometimes I wonder. We don't go to church, but he says he believes."

With my gaze holding hers, "I noticed on my printout that he is a Christian."

"Yes. But he won't talk about it. He says he's going to be OK. I think he may be angry that he's dying so young. He's only sixty-nine."

"So, he's been pretty private about his faith...." I glanced over to the patient, wishing he could speak for himself.

"Yes, never been one to talk much about deeper things..." David's eyes begin to open. "This is... What was your name again?"

I was grateful that God answered my unspoken prayer! "Pat."

"Yes, Pat. She's the chaplain." Surprisingly, the patient's son, who I thought was half asleep, stood up and slid the rolling stool over to me. I nodded my gratitude and sat down next to the patient.

"Hi, Pat. It's nice to have someone on this side of the gate." David was having a very difficult time talking and breathing at the same time. His voice was muffled and shot out in spurts, as the mask lifted slightly with his changing facial expression. I tried to read his lips as he continued to speak. No good. His wife, who had had more experience with this, repeated what he had just said to me.

He continued. "Brugin hip notter wit jar nif to..."

Oh, my. He was having such a difficult time that I felt that asking him to repeat himself would be torturous for him, so I decided to take a chance. I nodded.

David jerked off his mask. "Don't say that! I bet you didn't even hear what I said!"

Humbly, I responded, "You're right. I didn't understand it at all..."

David laughed and guffawed for several seconds. His eyes squeezed together as tears of laughter made their way through the tightened lids. I joined him and laughed at myself and the ludicrous situation.

David turned to his wife. "Could you get me some water?"

"Sure. Do you want me to leave, honey?" She handed him a cup half full of water.

"No." I was surprised by his response, thinking that since he did not openly discuss his faith with his wife, he would want to speak with me alone. Perhaps he wanted her to hear what he had to say but struggled to say it to her directly.

By this time, David's son had walked out of the room and into the hallway. I pulled in a little closer. "May I hold your hand?" As he assented, I took his hand in mind and gently held it, nestling it between my palms.

"Your hands are warm..." We sat in the silence and savored the blessedness of human touch. I waited for him to speak. "I do believe."

"You're a Christian."

"Yes."

"Are you at peace?"

"I am. Although sometimes I'm anxious. But I'm not afraid of dying."

"It's the unknown part on the way to dying that makes you anxious."

David nodded.

"I think that's pretty normal. Passing through 'the gate' is something you've never done before." I borrowed his phrase, keeping the imagery alive.

David nodded again.

Mrs. C stepped up and sliced her way into the intimacy. "Are you going to tell her about the...?"

David waved her away.

"Do you want me to go, honey?"

"No."

I sat by his bedside and waited. He looked a little stressed as he attempted to bring the water glass to his mouth and take a small sip. He put the cup on his tray.

"You know, David, I have as long as you need. I am not in a hurry. Take your time." I watched him visibly relax. The lines on his face melted away, and his body settled a bit deeper into his hospital bed.

"I think I've experienced angels or someone in my room these past two days. I was feeling anxious, and then I felt a warm hand on my left foot. I looked down, and there was no one there. The covers were over my feet, but I felt the pressure of the hand, sort of like your hand on mine right now. And then I felt peaceful. I knew it wasn't quite time to go..."

"Are those the words you heard?"

"Not with my ears. But in here." He pointed to his chest. "And then there was a second time. I was having a hard time breathing, and I was getting anxious, and then I felt a hand on my shoulder, but there was no one there. And then I felt peaceful again. Then there was a third time. The hands were shaking my shoulders, gently but firmly. I think I almost died that time, but then I felt peaceful again. There was no one in the room at the time."

I was amazed that he had the breath to share all of this with me. I smiled and gently rubbed his hand. "Just yesterday, David, I listened to a woman tell me that one time when she wasn't well, she opened her eyes and saw an angel lying across her bed looking at her. She described the angel in great detail."

David had put the oxygen mask back on, but I could see that he was grinning a huge banana smile. We spent several moments in silence.

"Is there anything you want or need to say to your wife or your son? Any unfinished business with anyone?" It seemed logical to me that if he had been prevented from dying, there must be a good reason. I wanted to help him discover what that might be.

He talked to me head on. "You mean bad stuff? No. Nothing."

"Good things? Like gratitude?" I probed.

"No, I've already said everything." By this time, his wife had left the room. I continued to wonder at his family dynamics—his need that desired presence but very little verbiage.

OK. I plowed straight ahead into the snowbank... "Earlier you mentioned that it wasn't quite time to go. Do you have any idea why?"

"Nope."

I waited for more.

"I think I'm done for now." His fatigue hardened into his torso and limbs, almost like he was a sculpture.

"It's been tiring for you to talk to me."

"Yes, but I wanted to. You never know when it's the last time."

"If you decide you want to talk more, let the nurse know. I'll be here a bit longer."

"What time is it?"

"About 4:30 p.m."

"OK. If I want to talk more, I'll just squeeze your shoulder." He grinned again underneath the mask. I quietly pulled the stool back from the bed and out of the way. His eyes were closed.

Before I left for the day, I walked by David's room. It was filled with people, almost as if a party was taking place, laughter, talking, hugging. I decided to continue walking and wondered why the touch of an angel had kept him here. What needed to be done or said before he walked through the gate? I'll never know for sure, but I can imagine that it had something to do with the people in that room. David died two days later.

God on Both Sides of the Equation

When I took the stool that David's son passed to me, it was a significant action. First, David's son was giving me a cue: You need to be here for my Dad. Secondly, being as close to eye to eye with a patient is extremely important. It conveys that we are on the same level. We are both human. Thus, we need to share this moment human to human.

When we care for others, we take chances. And when we are wrong, we might end up being embarrassed. That's simply part of risking love and care. I was hoping I did not have to ask David to repeat himself. He was having such a hard time breathing, let alone speaking. So, I took a chance. I guess I was baited and just didn't know it. I'm sure my face turned red. Better to admit my mistake and appear a fool! Thank God David had a sense of humor!

I've discovered that hand holding is always a sacred action. Asking first ensures that I have honored that person's personal space. Some people are not touchers. Better to ask first.

I was very deliberate in using David's imagery, "the gate." I knew it would build a bridge and also let him know that I understood what he was talking about. Using it felt right to me.

David needed to know I was not in a hurry. Even though I knew there were time guidelines for my consults, I also knew intuitively when someone needed more time. Where does that intuition come from? Perhaps it is the Holy Spirit working in me. Perhaps it is my empathic disposition. Or it could be a combination of the two. Non-verbal cues might figure into it as well—a person looking into the distance might imply that some thought is being given to something or someone, usually in the past. It might be the right time to ask if there is something else on the person's mind to talk about or share.

When I described the angel encounter of another patient (no names given nor any reference to a floor or hospital), it seemed to validate David's experience with angels. I am so grateful that David shared this experience with his wife. Though they might not have had many conversations about faith, this was one time that God could use the angel experience to give her some comfort.

Listening to Your Heart

- What does a listening stance or position look like for you?
- When you are listening to someone and misunderstand what is said, how do you handle being told, "You didn't hear what I said!" What kind of feelings might this elicit in the other person?
- Interestingly, David never asked "Why me?" I believe he had gotten beyond the question spiritually, maturing as he struggled with his illness. Most of the time, "Why?" is a useless question, and I deliberately choose not to respond to it. It seldom leads to deeper thinking. What questions might you ask that would lead the person to greater spiritual maturity?

CHAPTER 12
CHANGING LANDSCAPES

"...we are like a tree that has its roots in heaven and its branches down here."

—*J.B. Stoney*

A few months ago, my husband and I took a day to see the sights downtown. He had been working unbelievable hours, and we needed a day off together to relax.

We visited an urban mansion, a historic pottery store and even had the opportunity to attend a viewing of an historic baseball announcer, Ernie Harwell, in Comerica Park ball field, who had passed away at the age of ninety-two. He was a foundational part of many childhoods in the area. With transistors hidden under our pillows at night, we listened to ball games without the parental scrutiny of being up too late.

The last stop on our journey that day was to the area where my husband and I had met at church. I had wanted to see what the neighborhood looked like after all of these years. My grandparents had been founding members of the church and had lived down the block.

When we pulled into the street, I realized it was now a one-way street. I u-turned my way out of it and drove down the next road. There was the pub where my mother would take my hand to escort me around the stomach contents of some poor soul who had lost his dinner the night before. Today, it appeared to be a very popular spot in the city. Parking was no longer a problem, and the sidewalks were scrubbed clean.

The church was right around the corner—tiny compared to my memories of it, but well-kept with well-groomed lawns. And then I looked down the block... all of the houses were gone... every single one. Lush, long, green grass gently bending in the breeze now covered everything.

The houses of my childhood had been tiny, standing within feet of one another. Neighbors had been almost close enough to reach into each other's windows. Miniscule yards were manicured. The scent of burning tobacco was always in the evening air as people sat on their porches for a relaxing smoke before bed. Grandma and Grandpa had a standing invitation for us to come to their house after church every Sunday night for tea, cookies, and ice cream. Grandma's rose arbor arched over the gate to the alley. Ferns hugged the house. Hybrid teas spilled over one another in an effort to show themselves to each passerby. The alley to the north of the house opened up into a treasure trove of discards waiting for pickup the next day. On the other side of the alley, Grandma's vegetable garden covered an entire city lot—pregnant with vegetables too numerous to count or classify.

Inside the house, the kitchen with its bay window capturing scents of the roses tucked inside each little pocket of space, offered prime seats for people-watching down and across the east alley. As the mantle clock chimed in Westminster style, Grandpa offered his lap. And while his breath was not very pleasant, he shared Sen-Sen with me after popping a couple into his own mouth.(Sen-Sen was a tiny, licorice-flavored breath mint popular in the 1950's and 60's.) We looked at books together waiting for the tea kettle to sing.

The ice cream was always vanilla. The tea was always Red Rose. The cookies were always hard like our biscotti today. We would dip them into the tea and watch them soak up the tinted water and then allow them to dissolve in our mouths. It was luscious and comforting and stable. At least from my vantage point.

I used to go "alley-picking" with my cousin, but my mother would never allow me to bring any of my prizes home. I had to turn them over to my cousin and never saw them again. The only time I actually took anything home was when we found pennies in an old man's trash. This happened more than once. He burned his trash in the alley, and the pennies sparkled like diamond jewels in the ashes. I'm sure I had to wash them off with soap before I could put them in my pocket.

The landscape now rolled out before me. I saw no remnants of the life I once lived. The only hint that anything had existed on that block was a bit of concrete where the alley had been. All of the basements had been removed, filled in and erased from view. No glass, wood, or bricking remained. Nothing. Only my memories returned. I tried to superimpose them upon the land, but even my memory was incomplete and shaky.

When I stood on the front steps of the church, I pushed the buzzer to request entry, but no one responded. Either they had left for the day or saw us through the camera mounted on the corner of the overhang and decided not to bother with us. I peered in and saw the steps leading to the sanctuary, the door of the pastor's office that my husband and I had entered for our meager two pre-marital counseling sessions. We were now locked out and had to be at peace with that.

The young man in the Pediatric Unit was seventeen. He was due to graduate in the spring. He had been in an accident while driving a truck. A very severe accident. His life had seemed endless. He'd had massive ideas and places to go and people to meet. College was a dream come true and lay before him like the yellow brick road. He was on his way to Oz, never mind the man behind the curtain pulling levers. He was oblivious to the manipulations of the world. He was young, impressionable, and indestructible.

When I met him, he was unconscious, but his parents were not. They were stunned. They were huddled together like two children shaking in a thunderstorm without shelter. Stubble and pale cheeks betrayed them as adults. I walked into the room, knowing a little bit of what I was walking into. The nurses had whispered a few words into my ear before I entered the room. I was about to introduce myself to them, and before I had an opportunity, they held out their hands to me and implored, "Can we pray together?" *Their* landscape had abruptly changed, and they could not find their way home. What had once been a lush, generously rich family landscape was now barren. I cannot recall what I prayed except that I begged God on behalf of these two frightened people to have mercy on them and their son.

He lay in traction, his face bruised beyond recognition. His head was stabilized with pins and clamps. His internal injuries were numerous. We hugged and stood together talking softly. Other members of the family entered the room, and I excused myself so they could be alone with one another.

Several weeks later, I noticed that the patient was still on the Pediatric Unit. I had been filling in for another chaplain that first day, but today I thought I'd poke my head in, with her blessing, and see how he was doing. His eyes were half open. I walked to the side of the bed and spoke to him. He did not appear to respond. I touched his hand and spoke a silent prayer. When I talked to the nurses a few moments later, one of them told me that he had a severe closed-head injury, that he would probably never be himself again. The physical and occupational therapists were working with him. It was going to be a very long journey, and he would never be the same. Everything had changed.

I'm sure that Mom and Dad lingered over the memories of the son they had known. They rehearsed the scenery: his drive for adventure, the curve of his face that had sprouted facial hair, the way his hair hung across his forehead. They saw him jumping over fences, picking slivers out of his dirty hands, searching the house for his headphones, texting his girlfriend, waving good-bye as he pulled out of the driveway, the goofy way he looked at his sister to tease her out of a bad mood, his Facebook page littered with "trivial pursuits," his clothing scrunched into a ball in the corner of his room. And now, it was *gone*. Facial expressions that could be interpreted easily were now smoothed over by painkillers and broken circuitry. Agile limbs that rarely stopped moving were stilled, stiff, and stunted. Habits that had taken years to develop had been erased. For how many years will his parents' memories remain clear and lucid? Will the mourning ever end? What will be the "new normal?"

Sometimes listening is done purely with the heart. Few words are spoken; they are discerned. There are no answers, only questions, and none of them are answerable.

God on Both Sides of the Equation

How could I possibly relate to such a traumatic situation? Could my memories of a lost childhood dream give me any insight in the loss of the child this couple knew and loved? It might have been a poor representation, but it did give me a little insight into what used to be, what now is and the deep residual grief that resides in each one of us for a variety of reasons. I did not share any of these thoughts with the patient's parents. I really did not share any thoughts at all or even ask any questions. They would have been unable to hear or listen to what I might have offered. Anything that I might have said would have been so meager, like tossing a crumb into a vast ocean, swallowed up immediately with the power of the waves.

What did matter was my being there. I was not there to assuage their imagined guilt or relieve their pain or provide explanations of their process. Not at this time. I would have gotten in the way of their journey and taken them on a side trip that would have been unnecessary, even harmful. By being silent, I was hearing and listening to their needs. I was responding with something so significant that no one would be able to put a word to it except that my presence *mattered*. I was an impartial, non-blaming, non-problem-solving presence that helped to hold them up when they felt like shriveling into nothingness. Just as their presence was important to their son, even if *he could not* acknowledge it, so was my presence to them, even if *they did not* acknowledge it.

Listening to Your Heart

- Have you ever "been there" for another person in a tragic situation? Were you tempted to say something? Did you feel the pressure of having to come up with just the right words? I wonder what your presence meant to *them*.
- How do you relate to something devastating in another person's life if you have not experienced it yourself? Do you feel it is impossible to comprehend the depth of their pain? Do you need to understand it?
- What frightens you most about being with a person who has suffered a tragedy?

CHAPTER 13

THE GREAT EQUALIZER

"Lean on me..."

—*Bill Withers*

It was my fourth consecutive day on the hospital floor, and I was *tired*. Bone tired and emotionally limp, like an unwatered plant in the sun. There was a slew of people to revisit and a worship service to provide for the psych patients in 3Q.

I gathered the materials I had brought—handouts on responsive reading and the words to a song I intended to play—as well as a portable CD player with a plug-in speaker. I waited impatiently by the elevator, watching all four doors, ready to pounce into the one that opened first. And then I looked down and noticed that the key to let me into the ward was missing. My lanyard was not around my neck! Ah! I had left it hanging in the employees' restroom on a hook on the wall. And where was the key to the restroom? On that same lanyard! What to do?

Luckily, I was standing yards away from the security guard sitting behind the front desk. "Would you happen to have the keys to the employees' bathroom?" I pleaded.

"Yes, I do, Miss." *Miss! Don't you love it! I just turned sixty this fall.* He stood up, walked around the half-moon desk and over to the door to the restroom, then unlocked the door as he bent down, smiling up at me as he did so.

"Wow! Thanks!" I felt around the corner, turned on the light, and there was my lanyard, hanging on a hook right where I had left it. *Thank God!* And I meant it. I had exactly five minutes to get upstairs, let the nurse know I was present and set up. I grabbed the keys, locked the bathroom door, thanked the guard and flew into the open elevator, pressing "3" as I twirled around the corner.

As the door opened, I met the eyes of a physician who looked as if he had gotten up on the wrong side of the bed, if he had been to bed at all the night before. "Good afternoon!"

"Mmph," he grunted, as he slid into the elevator behind me.

Arriving at the first set of doors, I deftly slid in the key and turned it right. The double doors quietly unlocked. I pushed through them to the second set, turning the key in the next keyhole and noiselessly unlocking them. Usually, there was a unit orderly sitting just inside, but today the chair was empty. I strode quickly to the nurse's station. The charge nurse, Linda, spotted me and looked up. "You probably won't have many in the service today," she informed me. "We have more than our share of patients with psychosis today, and most of them are pretty non-functional."

"That's OK. We'll go ahead anyway." *Ever the optimist!* I had a clue that this might be the case since I had picked up the patient log the day before to prepare for the service: nineteen patients (all psychosis of one kind or another); sixteen Christian or non-denominational, two Muslim and one Jehovah's Witness. Working in a diversity setting, I always wanted to be sure that I custom-designed our services to meet the needs of everyone present—sometimes a challenging prospect. I figured that today we could read a Psalm responsively, and I had borrowed my husband's CD of

Josh Groban singing "You Raise Me Up," sort of a generic, spiritually uplifting song.

When I arrived in the activities room, the first thing I always had to do was to turn off the large screen television. I did this matter-of-factly, but I always expected someone to shout obscenities at me. (It hasn't happened yet, but that doesn't mean it won't!) So, on this day, I turned off the TV, rearranged the chairs in a circle of sorts, picked out a chair for myself, and sat down.

At the beginning of our services I would also put on some music to set the tone. That day, I chose meditative music, instrumental worship songs with some classical overlays. When I first came in, there were three individuals in the room. After I had the music playing, we progressively grew to ten. By the time I had whipped out the responsive readings and was passing them out explaining how they worked, two more patients came in and sat down. So, out of nineteen registered patients, we had twelve. I was impressed.

The responsive reading was Psalm 136. The repetitive phrase was "for his steadfast love endures forever." We began slowly, and I heard one or two voices. As we gained momentum, several others joined up, and we began to move along at a nice clip. I then noticed something rather odd. The young woman sitting across from me was smirking and muttering gibberish every time the group repeated the phrase. Now, if it hadn't been for the smirk, I might have thought she was speaking in tongues because that was how it sounded. Because there were so many speaking the phrase, it wasn't as disruptive as it could have been, so I just went along. (It's always a challenge trying to discern what to let go of and what to address in this unit!)

We completed the reading with everyone looking rather self-satisfied, as was I.

"I'd like to play a song for you now to wind up our time together, but before I do, let's pray." I said a short prayer, asking God to work out His ways in each of us.

It took me a few seconds to figure out the CD player since it was only the second time I had used it. The song began with a mournful violin, and then Groban's voice filled the room. I had passed out the words so the group could follow along. I leaned back and closed my eyes, thanking God for this unique opportunity.

Before long, I heard quiet sobbing. I looked up and saw Gina, the young woman across from me who had been smirking, holding a paper in front of her face. She was crying, and I could see her shoulders shaking. I decided to wait until the song ended before I would respond.

As soon as the song was done, I pushed the "off" button. "I usually play music at the end of each service. You are welcome to leave, or you may stay and listen to more music." A young man sitting in the corner ventured, "Can you play that song again? I really like that one."

"Of course I can." I pushed the button, and the violins began their slow climb to the measure with lyrics. Gina lowered the paper in adagio tempo, shifting it to her other hand. She gingerly stood up and raised one hand into the air, and then she began to point upward. It was one of those magical moments when the Spirit of God was moving, so I stepped over to her, slipping both of my hands into hers and together, we raised our hands to God. The papers she had been holding glided to the floor, and we held the pose until the song finished. I happened to notice that, when her shirt lifted slightly, she had stretch marks crossing her belly where one or two pregnancies had resided not too long ago.

Seconds later, she began to sob. I put my arms around her and held her close. As she rested her head on my shoulder, she whispered, "I just want to go home."

"I know you do," I whispered back, "but you have to get better first."

She drew away from me. "I'm sorry I cried all over you."

"No problem, Gina."

And then she smiled. I lightly touched her cheek.

"I like that," she whispered. I moved back into my chair and began to pack up. The woman sitting next to me, a self-proclaimed Methodist, said hesitantly, "When will things get better? This world is *so* bad!"

"Did you know that today is Christ the King Sunday? John writes in his book called Revelation that someday Jesus will put things right. We don't know how long it will be, but he will. Until then, we continue to anticipate God's kingdom growing and coming."

She smiled, looking relieved.

After everyone left the room, I walked down the hall and stood at the nurse's station. Patients swarmed around me like bees seeking nectar. Linda looked up from her endless paperwork. "Well, how did it go?"

"Really well," I said.

She raised her eyebrows. "Really? Well, what do you know!"

Yes, what *do* I know?

Well, I know that what I expect doesn't always happen. I know that I am often surprised. I know that wanting to go home has layered meanings, and I can't always assume that what is said is what is said. I know that God places each of us in particular places at particular times to serve God in particular ways—unplanned, unsought, sometimes unknown. I know that, because I am who I am, I miss so many of these opportunities because I tend to be consumed with my own thoughts, needs, and agenda.

I know that living in the moment means seeing what God sees as His eternal gaze pierces our temporal existence. I also know that the more I am open, the more opportunities to love one-on-one will sprout up around me because that's how God works.

I walked into the unit seeking to share some thoughts about gratitude since it *was* a few days before Thanksgiving. Instead, I received a graced occasion to love someone up close and personal, sharing the love that God has so extravagantly shared with me.

God on Both Sides of the Equation

Music is the great equalizer. It draws us in and puts us on a level playing field with others. In this case, God used music to touch the spirit of a young woman who had been burned by life. Because of her inability to cope in a healthy way, she was admitted to the Behavioral Health Unit.

In some ways, she had been the one unable or unwilling to listen. She blocked her feelings by being disruptive. The music I played came up against her walls, and one by one, the bricks began to fall until she reached above them to "touch the face of God."

I am so thankful that I did not say anything to her. The teacher in me wanted to call for help and have her escorted out. But God had other plans and coached me to keep still. I listened to her sobs. I saw her hiding her face from the rest of us, and then I was given full access to her as I joined her in praising God. This was a gift to her and a gift to me.

Remarkably, listening to Gina meant not paying attention to her words but listening to what she was *not* saying. Her actions, as they say, spoke much louder than her words.

I sometimes wondered if the young man who asked for the song to be played again was a "plant" by God! God knew that Gina wasn't finished and needed to hear more as she loosened her grip on her feelings.

Music transcends culture, age, religion, sexual orientation, financial status, and anything else we use to identify ourselves. Yes, we all have our favorite songs. But there is something about music that enters our soul and gives us freedom. It touches a deeper part of us that nothing else can touch.

One of the most meaningful things a chaplain can do is to play a person's favorite music when they are actively dying. Since hearing is one of the last senses to diminish, our hope is that the music will swell the soul as it passes from this life to the next.

Listening to Your Heart

- When was the last time you listened to music and felt touched by it? What effect did it have on you?
- Could music open up a conversation for you with someone you care about? If so, how?
- What if their favorite music does not appeal to you? Do you think it might be worth listening to gain a deeper understanding of that person?
- What do you think is meant by "listening to Gina meant not paying attention to her words but listening to what she was *not* saying?" Have you ever considered practicing this kind of listening?

CHAPTER 14
TWO PERSPECTIVES

The world and worldly things must be used with discretion, for without them life is not only difficult but impossible. For this very purpose God created the world that men might make use of it, but men should not drown themselves in it, for thus the breath of prayer is stopped and they perish.

—Sadhu Sundar Singh

"For now we see through a mirror, dimly, but then we will see face to face. Now I know only in part; then I will know fully, even as I have been fully known."

—I Corinthians 13:12 (NRSV)

To this day, I am still thrown off center when I recall what a patient shared with me as I was leaving his room one day in 2008. I was making rounds on a cold, cloudy afternoon, the kind where the clouds sit heavily upon everything and everyone like a weighted, damp blanket. I came upon a very unhappy man. This, in itself, was nothing new. Who wouldn't be unhappy lying in bed in the hospital with nothing to do, no privacy, and in physical and possibly mental pain?

"Hi, Mr. K. My name is Pat, and I'm one of the chaplains on this floor today. Just making rounds." I always added this since many people suspect that the only reason a chaplain visits is because the chaplain knows that the person is going to be handed a terminal diagnosis! However, in this case, I had reviewed his chart before I came in and knew that he was facing a very difficult time ahead.

"Oh, I'm OK."

This was going to be one of those times when I felt like I was trying to squeeze juice out of an apple by hand. "What is going on? You look terribly sad."

"I own a chain of stores, and I just lost a boatload of money."

I was surprised he didn't bring up his diagnosis, but then I realized who he was. I was standing in front of a billionaire. Here he was, hospitalized with a life-threatening illness, and foremost on his mind were his investments! He was riveted to the financial news and had passed off his diagnosis as a minor irritation. I knew I was skirting *his* main issue, but I just couldn't bring myself to discuss money with him, knowing what I knew. So, I went to my fallback position. "Do you have a faith tradition?"

"No, not really." Dead end.

"Family?" Before he could respond, we were abruptly interrupted, and I needed to exit the room to make way for the physician.

As I was leaving the room, he called after me, "Pray that I get all of my money back!"

How could I in good conscience do that? Instead, I found myself silently praying that this man would find a way to enter the kingdom of God in spite of his wealth. And I knew that his focus would need to change, his lens re-aligned so he could see clearly. Even though he was older, he appeared to be stuck in the first half of life issues–money, success, recognition. At the point of his powerlessness, I was hopeful that he would enter a conversion experience that would initiate him into a meaningful second half of his life.

During that same week, I visited a young man who had been in a motorcycle accident and was left paralyzed from the neck down. He had placed a request with the nurse to see me, and she had dutifully and electronically sent it to the Spiritual Care office. Since I was the one on call, I pulled it off the printer. I had just finished lunch, so I popped into the restroom and checked my teeth (always a good thing to do before engaging in a lot of smiling). No seeds, no spinach between teeth.

I straightened my lab coat and exited the suite. Getting onto the elevator can sometimes cause navigational problems. Someone had pressed "Down." I pressed "Up." In the time it took for me to turn around and notice that "Up" had surfaced before "Down," I missed getting through the door into the elevator even though I had cried out, "Stop! Wait!" Usually slow to arrive and patient to depart, elevator number three had pulled a fast one on me. If I didn't know better, I could easily believe that elevators had artificial intelligence and were programmed to tease their users!

When I finally arrived on the correct floor, I headed toward the nurses' station. It was always helpful to talk to the patient's nurse before entering the room if he or she is available. No nurse. Next best thing was to check the patient's chart. I sat down at the built-in desk outside the patient's room and pulled up his record. *Quadriplegic. This one was going to be a challenge,* I thought to myself.

I knocked on his door, even though it was open, just to be sure all was covered, and he was ready for visitors. He was sitting up in bed with a grin on his face, his mother sullen in the background.

"Hey, Chaplain, how are you today?"

"You can call me Pastor Pat, if you like. I think you stole my question!" I nodded to his mother to acknowledge her presence in the room.

"I was bored and needed to talk to someone."

"How are things going?"

"Well, let me tell you. I'm the poster boy for quads. You just wouldn't believe the opportunities I've had to talk to all kinds of people about what living in this body is like."

"What *is* it like?" Somehow the face and the demeanor just didn't fit the situation.

"I've been able to use it to help others. I figure that's why I'm still here."

"Hasn't it been difficult for you?"

"Well, maybe at first, but then I realized that other people need someone like me to cheer them up, and so that's what I've been doing." He then turned the conversation toward philosophy and theology. We verbally jousted a bit, and he looked satisfied.

I was ready to launch my zinger. "So, how does your faith tradition help you navigate this new life?"

"Well, I sort of tossed it out. It just didn't seem relevant anymore."

"What was your tradition?"

"I was raised Roman Catholic."

"Might I make a small suggestion?"

"Sure." He was all ears. Our conversation had given him enough knowledge about me to know that he could take what I said and seriously think about it.

"What would it look like to integrate your past faith into your present experience?"

"That's a good question. I'll think about it."

It was time for me to leave. One of the tough things about being a chaplain is the knowledge that we might never meet again. I would, once again, entrust this young man to the One who created him and wanted to use this experience to move in closer.

Weeks passed. Faces appeared and faded. Crises came in and went out like the tide. On a particular day, I was sitting at the suite computer looking over my patient list for the day, and I happened to see a name I recognized. It was the young quadriplegic man. He had come back in to have some wounds treated. I decided to poke my head in and see how he was doing.

I arrived at his door, knocked, and glided into the room. I was not prepared for what I saw. He was lying in bed and his face looked grey and withered. He looked downright depressed, and he was. His mother was again in the room, and she motioned for me to move outside with her.

"He is so depressed." she gravely shared. "I don't know what to do for him."

"Let me spend a few moments alone with him."

"Thank you. That would be great."

I walked back into the room and pulled up a stool next to his bed. He seemed like a different person. There was no energy to joust, hardly enough to have a simple conversation. "How are you today, Charlie?"

"Not so good. I'm really down." This was normal. This was healthy. He was out of denial and into truth. Not a pleasant place to be, but necessary. The beginning of healing.

And then I saw it. He had a rather large gold cross hanging around his neck. "I see a cross around your neck."

"Yes. I thought a lot about what you said. I decided that there are some things I learned that have been useful to me."

And I could guess what those things were: knowing that you don't suffer alone, that God suffers with you. Having a friend who doesn't judge you by how productive you are. Knowing someone who can see through all of your crap and still love you.

"I'm really tired. Thanks for coming by. I really valued our time together a few months ago."

Once again, I thought this was our last encounter, and in some ways, it was. A few weeks later, I received a card in the office mail addressed to "Chaplin Pat." The outside of the card had the Prayer of Serenity printed on it, and inside the card, he thanked me again for taking the time to invest in him.

Perspective. When God came knocking, he allowed God to change his perspective even though it meant sinking down into the depths of his soul into darkness.

Why are we so different? How can one be so closed and another so open? Perhaps it has to do with what we come to value and what, ultimately, gives our lives meaning. I will never forget the juxtaposition of these two dear souls.

God on Both Sides of the Equation

What might have happened if I'd had the time to be with the first patient longer? Might our conversation have led to a more meaningful outcome? Having to leave the room when the physician arrived was a bit frustrating to me. Obviously, he had unfinished business. However, isn't that where trust comes in? I was powerless to move the patient forward. Only God can do that anyway!

What questions might I have asked if I had been given the opportunity? I might have asked him how his illness fit into the fabric of his life. I might have asked if he had grown up with any faith tradition. I would have given him the gift of silence to further ponder my questions and the thoughts they evoked.

What about the young man who had quadriplegia? He was also avoiding his pain. His focus was on how he could use his disability to help others before he had even had a chance to fully come to terms with it.

Because Charlie was already open and searching, it had not been difficult to plant a few ideas into his thought process. I ask many patients, especially those who have had a faith tradition in the past, "How might going back and sifting through your earlier years of faith help you through what you are now experiencing?" Some patients want nothing to do with the past, for a variety of reasons. Others are not afraid to attempt to integrate those experiences into their consciousness.

Why was I not disappointed when Charlie came back depressed? Did I contribute to his depression? Initially, Charlie was moving too fast into his new life. This is not to say that ultimately he would respond in the same way, by helping others. However, based on my listening to his excitement over what he was doing, I realized that he had not yet felt any despair, sadness, or grief. His losses were unfathomable. He just didn't want to go there, but that is where true healing begins.

I'm not suggesting that Charlie wallow, and I certainly didn't want him to get stuck in unresolved and complicated grief. Facing the reality of his situation, along with the accompanying feelings, would bring positive movement toward healing and would ultimately allow God to use his experience to help others.

In one of these consults, I was not listening well. In the other, I was able to listen but realized that my input might bring about negative emotions. Sometimes that is the way it is. None of us are free from judgement or prejudice. Sometimes our listening will bring pain into another's life as we respond to what we see and hear. God can always use these types of experiences to help us grow.

Listening to Your Heart

- When have you turned away from someone and not listened because what they wanted to discuss was distasteful to you? How might you respond better so the person feels heard and cared for?
- When have you been hesitant to delve deeper into another person's sharing because you thought it might cause

negative emotions? Timing is everything. Would this person have been open to hearing you explain what you are hearing in their sharing?
- How do you deal with your errors in judgement when listening? Do you beat yourself up and then avoid people who bring out judgement in you, or do you think of it as a learning opportunity?

CHAPTER 15
MEDAL OF WORTH

"Through pride we are ever deceiving ourselves. But deep down below the surface of the average conscience a still, small voice says to us, something is out of tune."

—C.G. Jung

The page came unexpectedly given that I hardly ever received a page. What I heard so often was, "Oh, I should have paged you! Mrs. So-and-So really could have used your help." But the page seldom comes. I don't know if this is lack of training, lack of knowledge, or lack of communication.

So, when a page comes, I usually jump on it and call back quickly. "We have a patient in 6K2 who has requested a chaplain. No emergency, just come whenever you can come."

"I'll be up sometime today." Better to be a little nonchalant. This was not an emergency, and I didn't want to appear too eager. That gives me time in case I can't get there as soon as I hoped to. It takes the nervous anticipation away from the patient who might expect me to come charging through the door.

As it so happened, I did have several emergencies that day, and I finally made it up to 6K mid-afternoon. I unlocked both sets of doors, then strode quietly through the hallway and around the corner to check in with the nurse who had called me.

"I'm here to see Mr. Taylor."

"Oh, yes. I'll have one of the techs go get him."

"Do we have a private place where we could meet?"

"The patient conference room would work, but could you please keep the door open? We'll have someone circling the hallway to check on you and Mr. Taylor." That did not have a pleasant sound to it!

The unit tech rounded up Mr. Taylor, and introduced us to one another. "Borman, this is the chaplain." Borman grinned and held out his hand to shake mine. I briefly shook his hand and began to head toward the room set aside for private conversations.

"Nice to meet you, Chaplain. I need to talk to you."

Once inside the conference room, we sat down in chairs facing one another. I leaned slightly forward and looked into Borman's face. "What can I do for you today?" What deep dark secret might this man want to share with me? I have heard stories you wouldn't believe! I took a deep breath and silently prayed, *Lord, prepare me for what I am about to hear.*

"I just wanted someone to know that I am a genius!" I hoped my eyes were not betraying my surprise and relief. I was tempted to place Borman in a pigeonhole of schizophrenic proportions. Maybe a little affective disorder stirred into the mix. But I tossed my temptation aside and began to listen.

"I am from Liberia, have been in the United States for a few years and have done extensive reading," was how the conversation began. He got on the genius train and never disembarked until he had me convinced that he was right—he *was* a genius.

"Have you ever heard of or seen the movie called *A Beautiful Mind*?

He laughed. "Did you know someone told me I had a 'beautiful mind' just the other day, and we laughed about it. Yes, I have heard of the movie."

"You remind me of the main character." I wondered to myself if I should have been saying this. I was buying into his assertion. But I had to admit, the man was smarter than I will ever be!

We carried on a conversation that I would have never believed could have come from this unit. As he continued talking, his voice faded into the background. I began to think, *What is really happening here?* I have known extremely intelligent people, and why is it that many of them have to broadcast this fact to the rest of the world? Usually, there is a parallel deficit. So, they put forth the genius or Mensa label to mask their insecurity. Was this what was happening?

I took long strides to move alongside his train of thought once again and boarded the passenger car. "And I wanted to know, Chaplain, if you know the difference between depression and anxiety. The *textbook* definitions." Luckily, I was right beside him now.

"Well, I do know that anxiety is projection into the what-if's, and depression is a folding in... not exactly textbook but more experiential."

"That's right, Chaplain. But listen to this..." And then he launched into the most exhaustive definitions I have ever heard, bar none.

I wanted to get back on the right track. "Not to change the subject, but why, Borman, did you ask me to come to see you today?"

"Well, I just wanted you to know that I am a genius." And that was that. He was done, and I felt... what? Sadness at this waste of intelligence? Inferior because I did not possess an IQ of 160? I slowly came to the realization that this was his medal of worth. And he was honest about it! That's what I love about the Behavioral Health Unit—no masking, no passive aggression (it's all out there for everyone to see), and no beating around the bush. Everything is laid open. There is no false humility.

And then there was the time, I believe it was my first ever worship service in this unit, when I left feeling rather gratified. The man in the hallway who had decided not to attend the service called after me as I was leaving, "Thank you, Jesus! Good-bye, Jesus!" I was sorely tempted to believe that the Spirit of God was indeed hovering over me... until the next time I saw him. I had brought up a stack of Gideon Bibles for the unit and was on my way out. He called out after me once again, but this time it was, "Goodbye-mother-f! See you later, mother-f!" Definitely illness, *not* the Spirit...

Just this morning I met over coffee with a good friend. I can say just about anything to her and vice versa. Before we parted company, I hesitated. "Could I ask your advice?"

"You know you can."

"Do you think I should pursue commissioning? I'm trying to discern how I should be spending my time." I had the wrong degree, an M.A. instead of an M.Div., and this left me lacking. It didn't matter that my M.A. was in theology and counseling. So, I was in the process of taking a few denominational classes to shore up my understanding and practice of Reformed theology and practice so I could be commissioned as a ruling elder, a lay pastor of sorts.

"What attracts you to it? Why are you taking the classes? Or better yet, why did you decide you should pursue it? I mean, in the beginning?"

"Well, I thought it was what God wanted for me. I don't like the idea of presiding over meetings, but I love reading scripture, and I know I could preach a dynamite sermon. I think I have a pastor's heart."

"What really gives you life?"

"Hmm... I have to admit there have been times I have driven almost an hour for training during my chaplaincy internship and have been dog-tired by the time I arrived at the hospital. And then something really strange happened. By the end of the day, I was so energized, I was singing all the way home."

"And the church services?"

"When I assist, I feel... oh, I wish I didn't have to say this, but I know I can with you... I feel important."

Her eyes were a bit more penetrating than I am used to experiencing. She remained silent.

"I love it when people tell me that I'm a natural, that they love my voice when I speak and read, and then when they come out of the nave into the narthex, they shake my hand and tell me how much they appreciate me!" I looked down. "I hate being this honest, but I know it's good for me."

"I think you already know what you are supposed to do. You knew even before you asked me." Now, that's *genius*!

Self-deception is so easy. And hiding one's flaws really is the proper thing to do, isn't it? Why is it so blasted easy to get a higher opinion of ourselves than we ought to have? It almost makes me wonder if Satan told Eve how young and wickedly divine she looked before he smoothly laid out the temptation. A little flattery opens the door to so much more.

My dear friend shared with me that she feels pretty important, too, when she stands up in front of a group. Her job involves filling in for others as well as holding her own classes, and she eats up the praise. Why, she even notices that she might begin to feel a little bit of competition with the woman for whom she is filling in. Maybe she's even better than that woman. Who knew?

Borman is one of those people I will never forget. God chose to intertwine my conversation with him with my own discernment process. I'd like to be able to say that I have renounced my pride and resigned permanently from preparing for commissioning.

Well, you can guess what happened. I did get commissioned and then went on to be certified as a chaplain. Do I feel like a genius? Heavens, no! I do, however, feel that God directed my path, and I continue to learn new things about others and about myself in the process.

God on Both Sides of the Equation

What I learned from Borman was that each person is unique and each person is gifted. Whether or not I could classify that person as "normal" makes no difference. Even when a person is being treated for a mental health condition, he or she deserves to be heard and given the gift of listening.

The human tendency is to write people off because their logic is not our logic, and they may frame the world quite differently than I do. I am the one who loses when I discount a person's feelings and story simply because they have a mental illness diagnosis.

Is it really prideful to know what we do well? To know what our strengths are? Are we honest enough to know our deficits as well? If I am hesitant to share my deficits, leave it to someone else to pull them up and present them to me!

I had to laugh when the man in the hallway first compared me to Jesus and then, well, didn't. In some strange way, wasn't he being just doggone honest? One day, we can appear near perfect, and the next day, we bat zero.

I loved the questions my friend asked me. She was listening to me, and she was also gently assisting me to go deeper, even if it meant appearing prideful (which was really just giving myself a positive assessment on my better days). Part of listening is learning how to ask the right questions. I try not to paint myself into a corner by asking "Why?" Open-ended questions give the other person a lot of room for self-exploration, coming up with his or her own unique answer.

Listening to Your Heart

- Think about a time when you may have discounted someone because they don't think like you do. How could you have been a better listener? My guess is that there was some truth to what that person was saying. How do you separate the truth from the illness, or do you need to?
- Where do you find your "medal of worth?" Each person has unique gifts to offer. The world has a way of valuing gifts on a scale that is different than a spiritual scale. Recognizing and valuing another's uniqueness is really a holy act. Is there someone you know who could benefit from this kind of validation? Might you be using your own uniqueness to bring out this validation?

CHAPTER 16
LOSING CONTROL

"To be comforted by God is a promise that few of us ever receive, because we are consumed with controlling our situations to avoid being vulnerable."

—*E'yen A. Gardner*

It was several days before Christmas. I wanted to give my Behavioral Health Unit patients something, but I knew I would have to be careful. Unfortunately, the Unit is quite stark for this reason. One never knows when and with what a patient might try to harm herself or another. I, for that reason, have been handing out pictures—crocuses in the snow, sunrises, nautilus shells. Imagine receiving something so beautiful to gaze at when reality is far away or peace is elusive. I also offer an accompanying scripture if one chooses to take a copy. Most of our patients happen to be Christian, but not all.

Two weeks ago, I carried two copies of the Quran to the floor, and they were held close after I passed them out to two young Muslim men who were in their rooms. Another patient passed by me as I was giving them away. "Do you believe that stuff?" I chose to remain silent. I don't think one has to 'believe that stuff' to be kind, show love, and embrace hurting people.

I decided to call up to the unit before I went out to buy something for the patients for Christmas. "I don't have a clue," the case manager said. She held the phone away from her mouth. "Do any of you know what would be a good gift for our patients for Christmas?" I heard in the background, "No sugar, please!"

That sort of nixed my first idea—chocolate. Who doesn't love chocolate?

"Well, if we come up with something, we'll let you know." Cards. I could give them each a card. That would be both safe and meaningful.

The phone rang minutes later. "How about oranges? You know, those little ones, what are they called? You know... clementines?

"That would be perfect! I'll do it!"

It was a very busy week, and the only time I had to go out and search for clementines was Sunday morning, two hours before the service. I not only had to find them. I wanted to wrap each one individually and tie them up with a ribbon (a very short ribbon). I had to miss my own church service to pull this off.

The first store was close to home and had become our back-up when we needed something quick. A bit expensive, but time is worth money, too. I weaved my way into the produce section looking for those cute little oranges. All I could find were clementine imposters! They were called clementines, but they were about double the size. No, they just wouldn't do.

I hurried out of the store, unlocked the car and sat for a few minutes in the seat wondering where in the world I could find the *right-sized* clementines. I knew there was a gourmet market a couple of miles away. So, I headed in that direction, looking at the clock in the car and getting a little tense.

I pulled in, parked, then sloshed through the snow, grumbling about having to wait so long for the automatic door to open. I careened around corners searching for the orange aisle. Ah, there they were. A sign advertising clementines hung high above the bin. As I moved closer, I felt as if a conspiracy was working against me. Oh, sure. There were the clementines. The overly-large oranges shabbily disguised as cute clementines! A store employee (or so I thought) approached me. "Can I help you?"

"These clementines are too big!"

"You sound upset!"

"I'm taking these to my patients on the psych unit, and I really wanted smaller ones..."

"How many do you need?"

"Twenty."

"Let's look through the bags and see what we can find."

Really? I thought. *You're going to take the time to open up some of the bags and pull out any little ones you can find?*

"Well, they're not little, but there are at least eighteen or twenty per bag. Will that do?"

"I just counted a bag, and there are only sixteen. I can't afford two bags of these things!"

"Well, (he rips open a bag) here are five more. Will that be enough?"

"Wow, thanks!"

"Tell the checkout clerk that Tony said these are all free."

Can this really be happening to me? I checked out, rushed to the car, drove quickly (too quickly) home, pulled out the tissue paper and ribbon and began wrapping twenty-one rather large clementines. I put them into a fabric shopping bag, along with some meticulously weighed bags of chocolate covered peanuts for the staff, then jumped into my car and headed out.

Overloaded as usual, I parked in the underground garage, managed to slide into the elevator making my way to the revolving door at the front of the hospital. It's a quirky door. If one moves too fast, the door gets confused and stops. If one moves too slowly, the door gets impatient and keeps moving, shaming the waiter into waiting for the next opening. You can probably guess what happened to me!

I finally made it into my office, changed the pagers to in-house, swiped my card into the time clock, then removed my winter wear to get ready for the worship service upstairs. Heavily laden, I took the elevator to the third floor, keyed myself in, and walked quickly to the nurses' station. "The service will begin in ten minutes," I announced. Ten minutes. Those ten minutes are precious. I got organized, found the plug for the CD player, chose a chair for myself, and turned off the large screen television. Then, I begin playing music. Ah, music—the great equalizer. Today, we had Christmas music.

The theme for this service was Advent, the 4th Sunday, and the scripture passage was Matthew 1:18-25, the story of Jesus' birth. We only had five patients this time. It was a little disheartening. I had gone to so much work for this service. But that's the price I pay sometimes for being too organized and in a hurry. I wear myself out for no good reason!

I passed out the song sheets, along with the scripture passage printed on parchment paper. Everyone loves parchment. It has a great feel and an even greater look. One patient was sitting back in his chair muttering. As I got closer to him, I could hear him say, "You are a control freak. You need to relax. It's people like you who get their undies tied up in knots." *Did I really hear that? Is this patient* psychic, *too?*

We read through the scriptures, one verse at a time, taking turns. And then we began to sing a Christmas carol together: Silent Night. Meanwhile, Mr. R continued his litany: "You are such a control freak. The world has too many of you..." We began the second verse, "Silent Night, Holy Night, Shepherds quake at the sight..." Mr. R joined in this time, and I was relieved. It's difficult enough to keep everyone in sync, but when there's background noise, it's especially challenging.

After the second verse was sung, I continued to play the instrumental music and began to pass out oranges. The patients were elated. Sweet and seedless (in spite of their size!). I finished passing them out. It was then that Mr. R came up to me with his hand out. Immediately, I said, "No, Mr. R. you can only have one orange." He backed up for an instant and then retorted, "I only wanted to shake your hand to say thank you for the orange." The other patients followed his lead, each one saying thank you and shaking my hand.

I gathered my things and worked my way back to the nurses' station. I then passed out the chocolate covered peanuts to each person behind the desk. I wondered if anyone ever remembered the staff. They were so grateful for such a small gesture.

I left the unit that day feeling unusually humbled. How had Mr. R pegged me before I even opened my mouth? I relayed the story to my sister, Dianne, who lives in Tennessee, the following morning. When I finished telling the story, she could hardly speak because she was laughing so loud and long.

"I wish I could have seen you in the supermarket bemoaning the oranges. Maybe the manager thought you were the one under psychiatric care, and he just wanted to get rid of you as soon as possible!"

I think she was laughing because she knew. I knew. She knew me, and I knew her. And we have a lot in common having been raised by the same mother.

Underneath all of the laughter and humility, I remember hearing, "Did you get it?"

Yes, Lord. I got it.

God on Both Sides of the Equation

Do you recall my sharing earlier about loving to work on this floor because honesty was quite prevalent? People usually say exactly what they think and don't hold back. Mr. R was a prime example of just that. My organizational skills came with a deficit. When I am too organized, too in control, I miss things. I don't see people as well as I need to. I don't really hear what's behind the truth being shared. Yet, truth shines in the most unlikely of places through the eyes of a person who saw what he saw and felt the need to share it. Aimed at me, it was the truth, and I could not deny it. I was trying to do something nice for my patients, and what did I get in return? Some very heart-felt thanks and a bit of pure, unadulterated honesty. I also came away from the encounter, after much thought, knowing that my ego needed adjusting. I wanted so much to appear "nice." And now, that image was blemished!

After Mr. R spoke up, I had his number, and at that point in time, I did not trust him. I knew, just knew that he was going after a second orange. How I misjudged him! But isn't that what we all do? Someone shares something or does something hurtful. Instead of pulling the truth from what was said or done and then tossing the rest away, I sit in judgement and mistrust. How many times have I gone back into my past only to find that someone did something "unforgivable," and from that moment on, I avoided that person? There was no fixing it, the person never apologized, and here I sit today with regret that I didn't handle things differently. Just when I think I am being loving and giving, I come up against my weaknesses. In some ways, I really needed to thank Mr. R. Not many people are that honest. He gave me a chance to grow and change.

Listening to Your Heart

- How many times have you planned something that you thought was absolutely wonderful, only to be brought up short? The wind was taken out of your sails, and you wondered if it had been worth the sacrifice. Was your plan more important than your presence? How could you have

seen this differently at the time? What might you have done differently?
- Is it ever appropriate to agree with someone who is judging you? What do you think would happen if you did? How might the relationship change?
- I heard what Mr. R said, but did I really listen? Not at the time. I misjudged instead. How does judgement affect your relationships? How might you be able to think and act differently?

CHAPTER 17
THE POWER OF VALIDATION

"I've learned that whenever I decide something with an open heart, I usually make the right decision..."

—Maya Angelou

A call came through to our office at the front end of the day. "There's a patient on your floor who wants a priest," Jacob said.

"Maybe I should call the floor and find out if it's an emergency first," I responded back as I continued to check my emails. So, I got on the phone and asked. After I got the reply, I communicated back to the chaplain who was handling priest connections for the day. "No emergency. I'll see him later in the day and tell him that a priest will be in tomorrow."

I continued to work on my visit list, adding this man to the list, anticipating that I would see him early afternoon.

After lunch, I made my way up to the floor. I decided to read his chart just to be prepared for what I might see and hear. Then, I made my way over to the hand sanitizing dispenser, walked in and asked if the patient would welcome a visitor.

"Sure, come on in."

Roy was sitting in the chair next to his bed. I could see he was a very large man even though he was seated. Not obese but tall and big. His face was a little splotchy, probably due to a skin infection, and his hair was white and thinning. There were no notes or flowers in his room. In fact, it was rather stark.

"Hi, Roy. I'm Chaplain Pat. I heard you wanted to see a priest today. Unfortunately, we don't have a priest in house right now, but I could put you on the list for tomorrow. Is that OK?"

He answered quickly, "Sure." As I looked at him, I thought I detected a need for company. He wasn't smiling and was a bit hunched over. "OK if I sit down for a few minutes and talk with you?"

"I'd like that." He looked up at me with pale blue eyes. One lid was drooping. A life of sadness surrounded his gaze. I opened the closet, pulled out a chair and sat down in front of him. The tray table stood between us, and he leaned on it now and then.

"Tell me a little about yourself, Roy." He began to share about his past and the fact that he had cerebral palsy due to physical abuse by his father. His siblings had somehow avoided the violence that caused Roy's infirmity, but they had also been abused, and left home angry and determined to make something of themselves. In fact, all of them were wealthy and had an abundance of homes, boats and other symbols associated with wealth. Several lived out of state.

Roy lived in a facility and could no longer walk. He was confined to a wheelchair. Having suffered several TIAs in the past few months, he was back in the hospital to find out if he'd had another one.

I listened, and what I heard broke my heart. *How can life be so cruel? How much can one person bear?*

I asked him about his faith. Since he was Catholic and had wanted a priest, I thought this was a fair question. "Does your faith help you through these hard things?"

"I'm not even sure God is around. I don't feel like He cares about me."

"Sometimes it certainly feels like that. Do you have any friends? People you can trust?"

"Yes. I do have some AA friends. I have a sponsor whom I talk to now and then." He looked down. Tears formed in the corner of his eyes and began spilling down his cheeks. He took a few minutes to wipe them away and then appeared to have a hard time swallowing.

"Would you like me to get your nurse to see if I can give you some water?"

"Please." I checked with his nurse, and he could have nothing by mouth until his tests were over. I relayed this information to him.

He continued to clear his throat and swallow and kept apologizing for the delay in his responses. I waited silently. When he had collected himself, I ventured, "What are the tears about?"

"I'm not sure. I haven't cried for years…"

"You have a lot of stored up sadness. It's a healthy thing to cry and release those feelings."

His hands began to shake. "There's something else. I don't know if I should tell you. There could be a lawsuit over this. Do you promise not to tell anyone?"

"Our conversations are absolutely confidential. Even when I write my notes, I will say nothing about the content of our conversation, only that you appeared sad and anxious," I wanted to give full disclosure.

He hesitated. And then hesitated some more. I was already determining that there were psychological issues present. And no wonder! This man had been through so much. Had been abused, belittled, neglected, and scoffed at.

"I have a secret," he whispered. "I have a liver tumor. Every time I tell someone, they don't believe me, but it's there. The doctors have run tests, and they can't find it, but I know it's there. Do *you* believe me?"

I had a choice. I had already looked at his chart. There was mention of a liver tumor but that his CR scan was clear. *Do I tell him that I believe him or do I question him? What was the loving thing to do?*

"Yes, I do believe you. That must be a very frightening thing." His anxiety was through the roof. He continued to talk about his fear of the future.

I was hoping that what I wanted to do next would not minimize his fears but actually give him an out and empower him. "Roy, what would it feel like to let the past be, put the future in God's hands, and live in the present?"

"That's exactly what my sponsor said to me not too long ago."

Phew! My gamble paid off! Thank God! "What is happening in the here and now that might give you hope?"

"You being here."

"Aww, I appreciate that."

"You have given me hope. I feel better somehow."

Simple listening and validating can hold so much power...

"You know, Roy, you're not in this life alone. God has brought people into your life who care about you. Those tears that you cried today were not only tears of sadness but could be an evidence of the Holy Spirit touching you. Many people feel emotional when the Spirit comes to them, loving them."

He listened to what I said. He didn't say anything in response, but he heard me.

"I would like to bring you a gift. It's called a love blanket. We bring these to patients who need to know they are loved. Would you like one?"

He smiled for the first time in the hour I had been sitting across from him. "Yes, I would."

"What is your favorite color?"

"Blue or purple. I really like both colors."

Later, I dropped in to see him before I left for the day. I had found a blue plaid fleece blanket. After I placed it over him, he remarked, "I was cold, and now I'll be warm." I waved goodbye and left the room. As I was washing my hands on the way out, I thought, *So much truth in those words.*

God on Both Sides of the Equation

Here was a hurting man. His past had scarred him almost beyond recognition. His family had not been caring for him, and he believed God was distant. He did mention a sponsor from AA that filled in the picture a bit more for me. It could have been that his family wrote him off as a "drunk." Even so, his loneliness was thick and unsettling. It drew me in to dig a little deeper.

Roy was convinced that he had a liver tumor. His medical records did not reflect his conviction. He'd had a wealth of tests, and nothing like a liver tumor had showed up. So, why in the world would I agree with him? Sometimes validating a person's beliefs are more a sign of love than telling the truth. If I had told Roy the truth, how would that have affected our relationship? Would he have felt cared for?

By pulling Roy into the present moment, he was able to see goodness. He was able to experience God by not dwelling in the past nor being anxious about the future. It was a very sacred moment in time. Hope was present, and Roy felt loved.

Listening to Your Heart

- When someone unloads their hurts while revisiting the past, how are you affected? Do you tend to become emotionally overwhelmed? Is it easier to jump into the rapids with them and then try to console them? What might happen if you were more emotionally removed and asked a few questions instead?

- Is it possible to be "with" a person and still give yourself permission to separate yourself emotionally? How does that feel to you?
- Do you feel you always have to "set things straight?" Is truth more important than love?

CHAPTER 18

THE STILL, SMALL VOICE

"Blessed are you, Lord God, maker of all living creatures. You called forth fish in the sea, birds in the air and animals on the land. You inspired Saint Francis to call all of them his brothers and sisters. We ask you to bless this pet. By the power of your love, enable it to live according to your plan. May we always praise you for all your beauty in creation. Blessed are you, Lord our God, in all your creatures! Amen."

—From Franciscan "Blessing of the Pets"

On another busy day, I was charting my patient notes when I felt a gentle tap on my shoulder. I glanced up and noticed Suzanne, one of our volunteers standing beside me.

"I just came from the ER. While I was loading the comfort cart with blankets, I noticed a couple in one of the rooms. They called out to me and asked me if I could get a hold of a chaplain for them. Could you go? They're in pod 36."

"Of course. I laid down my pen, picked up my note binder and walked back to the ER. After waving my badge in front of the doors, I was allowed in and headed for pod 36. When I walked in, a man in his forties was sitting up in the bed looking a little peaked.

"Hi, I'm Chaplain Pat. I was told you wanted to see me?"

Mr. Tyler said, "My wife is very upset."

That seemed odd to me since he was the one admitted to the ER.

"We wanted to have our dog blessed. She meant so much to my wife."

I could understand her feelings. I have two dogs of my own, and their faithfulness and emotional IQ went beyond any human's ability to intuit.

Mrs. Tyler began to tear up. "Our dog just died," her voice cracked. "He's in the trunk of our car... this has been an awful day. Now my husband is in the ER."

My mind tried to make sense of what I was hearing. I turned to Mr. Tyler, "What brought *you* into the ER?"

"I was in quite a bit of pain. I guess I have kidney stones," he grimaced.

"Why don't I pray for you?" I ventured. They agreed, and I did.

"Can you bless our dog?" his wife asked again.

"I'm not sure that would..."

"That's OK. I just needed to ask."

I wrapped things up and sat down outside his pod to chart my notes. As I was charting, I heard a very clear mandate in my heart. "Bless the dog." *Really?* I kept charting. Once again, I heard very distinctly within, "Bless the dog." I finished my charting and headed back to Mr. T's pod.

"I've thought about it, and I've decided I would love to bless your dog."

Mrs. T looked up with a tear-stained face. "Really?"

"Yes."

She led me out to her car in the emergency lot and lifted the lid of the trunk. There, in the center of the trunk, was a small, dog-sized box with a lid on it. All around the box were flowers, several bouquets, in fact.

"We were on our way to the vet to have her put down. She had been so sick, and we decided it was time. She was fifteen years old. Before we could get to the vet, she stopped breathing, and then my husband started having pain in his side. We had to come here before we could go home." She gently lifted the lid.

There was a little black and white dog, laying on her side, wrapped in a crocheted blanket. A blanket someone had made with pure love. I placed my hand on the dog. "She's still warm," I noted out loud. I prayed with my hand on the dog, thanking God for her and the goodness and blessings that she had brought to this family.

When I ended my prayer, Mrs. T looked up at me and said, "Do you see the blanket that's wrapped around my dog?"

I nodded.

"That was my babies' blanket. We were in an automobile accident thirteen years ago, and both of my babies were killed. I wanted Dorothy wrapped in the blanket when we bury her in the yard."

There was a rush of recognition that moved from my head to my heart. I wrapped my arms around her and held her while she wept. "If it hadn't been for that dog, I would have died from sorrow. She kept me alive." My tears were beginning to flow as well.

If I hadn't listened to the *voice,* I would have never known this. I would have missed an opportunity to allow Mrs. T to grieve as she needed to grieve. I would have missed another lesson in listening to the still, small voice of God within me.

God on Both Sides of the Equation

From childhood, we are taught or have modeled for us a life of protocol. We should do this, say this, be this. We shouldn't do this because... and on and on. When we are unable to shake the protocol, we lack the freedom to do things differently in a way that might *really* make a difference. My husband laughs at me when I insist on crossing the street at a crosswalk. Now, as I've grown older and wiser (maybe), I do break this rule now and then when I know it would not be dangerous. But the rule has been firmly embedded in me, probably since my early days: "You must only cross the street at a crosswalk!"

I know there are reasons for rules and keeping things in their proper place. When the rules override love and compassion, I have to wonder if I am more afraid of reprisal than anything else. I have been reading *With Open Hands* by Henri Nouwen. The last chapter of the book explains the revolutionary characteristics of Jesus, who was able to view the rules as guidelines but never placed them over the needs of people. Sometimes, with my need to be loved and cherished, I adhere to the rules because I don't want to be challenged or judged harshly.

What was the rule I was breaking, anyhow? Something like, "If you walk out of the hospital into the parking lot and place your hand on a dog, you might bring germs into the hospital that could harm someone." Was this written anywhere? Perhaps it was simply "common sense."

I am not used to hearing the voice of God so insistently. Usually, I get a nudge or a thought that flickers through my spirit guiding me to consider something. This was different. Apparently, I was missing the point, and God wanted to make sure I got it right! So, I heard the words within myself—not once but twice. I'm thankful I was listening. There was something important that I was not meant to miss, both for my sake and for the sake of the woman who requested the blessing for her dog.

Listening to Your Heart

- Have you ever thought you heard the voice of God within you but dismissed it? Perhaps you thought it was simply your own thoughts. What might have happened if you had responded to that voice? What might you have done differently?

- Are you a rule-keeper or a rule-breaker? What motivates you to be that way? Have you become more rigid or flexible in those tendencies?
- Are you able to look beyond the rules and see something, perhaps, more vital than keeping them? Can you think of an instance when this was true for you?

CHAPTER 19
OF PATIENCE AND CONNECTION

Do not consider then, however learned you are, that your knowledge is complete. For learning is the river of G-d and we drink of it throughout our lives.

—*Rachel Kadish*

Michael was devastated. He had lived a risky life even though he was raised as a Christian. At the peak of his drug-of-choice lifestyle, he had a stroke that affected his right side. He could no longer use his right hand.

"When *I* touch my arm, I can feel it, but when someone else touches it, I can't."

Of course, he was right-handed.

When I first met him, he was in a wheelchair surfing the hallways on his floor. The rooms were arranged in a circular fashion, and he found it invigorating to wheel himself around and around and around. When I asked him how he was doing, he said he was OK.

"I'm used to bicycling. I just can't sit still and wait for things to happen. I need to be on the move!"

When I met him the second time, he said he was feeling down. When I finally entered his room and saw him for the third time, and we talked at length, he admitted to being very depressed.

"Tell me about your life, Michael. What has had meaning for you up to this point? Do you have any particular faith tradition?"

He had to think for a few moments as if he was stuck in a hole and was unable to see daylight. He also found it difficult to speak.

"Well, when I was growing up, my mom ran a pretty tight ship. Sometimes I felt she was too hard on me. She was a Christian and spoke in tongues. But she loved me, and I had no doubt of that." He did not mention his father.

These conversations were long and drawn out since Michael's stroke had affected his speech. Sometimes the wrong word came out, and he would shake his head in frustration. Then he would start again. I had to be *very* patient which is not one of my strengths. In some ways, I am just like Michael. Even with all of my training, I have to slow myself down inside and do a lot of waiting, which can be challenging since the other side of my personality just wants to get things done!

"She was hard but good."

"You speak of her with sadness in your voice."

"I'm really sorry that I was not with her before she died. There was so much I wanted to say." He looked away from me.

"Tell me about that time."

"Well... she had liver failure."

My first thought was, *She was an alcoholic,* but he then immediately corrected my thinking as if he knew my very thoughts. "She took too much Tylenol. I guess she was in a lot of pain, but it destroyed her liver. She was getting so sick, and I was in prison. It was my own fault, and I couldn't be there for her. I've carried that guilt for years." He looked over at me, eye to eye. "I've never told anyone about this. You are the first one."

The sacredness of that moment was almost overwhelming. His mother had passed away over twenty years ago.

"You've been carrying a heavy load for such a long time…"

"Yeah. I just feel so bad."

I see this often. A person enters the hospital with something so life-changing that, as they sit in their room day after day (and sometimes week after week), they have time to think. Many scenarios and memories come to the surface. It is a vulnerable time, but it can be incredibly productive.

"From your past, when your mother was alive, do you remember the story of Peter? When he betrayed Jesus?" I summarized the story for him, and he seemed to remember. "Peter was ultimately forgiven and became a free man. Not only that, he grew into a mature, dynamic disciple who shared the good news with many. Catholics believe that he was the first bishop of Rome, a predecessor of the popes. Can you imagine denying Jesus three times and then being forgiven for everything? Not only that, but elevated to being called 'the Rock'?"

He looked me in the eye again. "Didn't he feel guilty?"

"I imagine he did, but I guess he figured that if Jesus could forgive him, he also needed to forgive himself."

He sat in silence. He knew what I was saying. I could see by the way he was gazing that he was reaching deep within.

I continued. "Do you believe that your mother forgave you?"

"I hope so."

"What about God? Does God forgive you?"

"I think so."

"That leaves only you… forgiving yourself. You have to know that most of the time, we need help doing that." I thought carefully before self-disclosing my own misstep to him. "When my mother died, I was not with her. I had told her that my sister would be on her way up from Tennessee the next day, and I fully expected her to remain alive until she had seen my sister. I went home and went to bed thinking I would have at least another day or two. I was wrong. She died around 6:00 a.m. the following morning, and the assisted living facility called me at 8:00 a.m. She had already been gone for two hours. I missed saying goodbye, and I never had taken the time to tell her how much I appreciated all she had given to me throughout the years…"

He winced. "Do *you* forgive *yourself?*"

"For the most part, yes. But sometimes I still feel regretful. I have to remind myself that God has forgiven me. She has forgiven me. The only one left is me, and God continues to help me with that. Every time I think about my mistake, I lift it up to God and try to leave it there."

He was silent, looking down at his hands. "You remind me of my mother." I offered to pray with him, and he was open. I placed my hand on his knee and prayed that God would help him forgive himself and set him free from his own guilt so he could live the life that God was calling him into.

"It looks like I'll be leaving on Friday." He had been in rehab for almost three weeks.

"Tomorrow is my last day here this week," I shared. "May I come back tomorrow and leave you with a blessing?"

"I'd like that."

I went back to the office, found a Gideon New Testament, located some verses that I thought might be helpful to him and wrapped a sparkly white ribbon around it.

The following day, I looked for him. He was out and about again. A woman I did not know was also looking for him, and we connected. I thought it might be his sister.

"No. I'm from the Time Bank." The Time Bank is a way for residents to share their needs and gifts with one another. Michael was needy. He would require someone to look after him until he could care for himself. He had begun walking again but was a bit unsteady. He had a sister, but she was not in the best of health and had decided not to come visit him while he was in rehab. He was so disappointed.

"I'll come back a little later to see him. You go ahead." I said.

About an hour later, I came back to his floor, and they were still talking in the family waiting room. I hated to interrupt, knowing how frustrated I feel when someone interrupts my visits, especially when we are breaking new ground and deep into processing feelings, thoughts, or attitudes.

She looked up at me. "Did you need to talk with Michael?"

"Is it OK if I give him a blessing? It's short, and I promised him I would do this before I leave for the day."

"That would be fine."

"Is this time OK, Michael?" I asked.

He nodded. He turned to face me in his wheelchair. I placed my hands on his shoulders. "May the Lord bless you and keep you safe, Michael. May he make his face to shine upon you and be gracious to you, helping you forgive yourself. May God give you His peace from this day forward." *(slightly edited version)*

We said goodbye to one another, and then he turned back to the woman sharing resources with him. I walked away and down the hall. I thought about the words I had written in his Bible, "Michael, thank you for sharing your life with me. God continues to want to heal you in every way possible, especially the guilt you carry. May you lift it up to Him every time you feel it so that your load will be lighter. God has something in mind for you. He will use you to bring healing to others if you allow it."

This is my story as well!

God on Both Sides of the Equation

With Michael, it took three visits to hear his real story. The first time he was "OK." The second time, he noted that he was feeling down. The next time, he admitted to being depressed. Sometimes it takes more than one encounter to hear the "real story." Perhaps it's a matter of trust or it may simply be a matter of timing. Maybe Michael did feel OK and that deteriorated to feeling very depressed as time went on. It was a reminder to me to not give up on a person. Sometimes it takes more than one connection to earn the right to be the listener.

I have a limited supply of patience. I'm better at being patient now than I used to be, but sometimes it is still a struggle. Ever hear the adage, "Don't pray for patience!" God hears that prayer and then sends you opportunities to practice! Patience is also an invitation to slow down. When I move at a good clip, I know I miss things. When I am forced to slow down, the scenario will gently unfold in front of me, and I am able to see and experience beauty disguised as pain. This was Michael. He was in great turmoil, but at the same time, he was regretful, and I could see that he loved his mother very much.

When I took the time to listen to Michael, I could reflect back to him not just what I heard but what I saw. Being with a person "in person" allows a beautiful flow of communication–both spoken and unspoken–that when woven together, gives the listener a clearer view of what is really happening within the other person.

I did something on this visit that I rarely do. I shared something out of my own experience of guilt. While this could have turned the focus on me and drawn it away from him, I took the risk. And I was very glad I did. He could see that I was just as human as he was and had some of the same struggles. Not only did it bring us closer together, but it also took the stigma of guilt and deflated it for him. It was even good that he challenged me, asking me if I had been able to forgive myself. We discovered together that both of us are a work in progress.

Listening to Your Heart

- Have you ever connected with a person who was "OK," but you did not believe them? What happened?
- When was the last time you said you were OK but you really weren't? How did the other person respond? Did you wish they would have responded differently?
- There are times when sharing your own story takes the focus off the other person. What made it effective in this circumstance?
- When you are sitting alongside someone, do you notice more than just their words? Try doing this sometime and see what comes of it. Do you gain a better understanding of that person? Do their words and their tone or stance contradict one another? Which do you trust more?

CHAPTER 20
ERASING LIFE

Over the years your bodies become walking autobiographies, telling friends and strangers alike of the minor and major stresses of your lives.

—*Marilyn Ferguson*

I was brushing my teeth one morning when, as the news came on the television in the kitchen, my ears were drawn to the story being told.

"*A controversial trial in which a young woman is charged with killing a police officer is now in the hands of the jury...*" With an electric toothbrush in my mouth, I made my way around the corner of the bathroom and into the kitchen. "Ms. Penski is charged with first-degree murder in the December 28, 2008, death of twenty-eight-year-old Officer Manuel Rivera. The jury entered their second day of deliberations on Thursday..." With toothpaste dripping from the corner of my mouth, I remembered...

A few days after Christmas, I was on call. During the holiday season, I had signed up to be on call for several shifts to help out. Some were completely uneventful, which is rare. Others were busier than I wanted to be. This particular night, a call came from Trauma. I dialed the extension and listened. "Please come down to the Emergency Center. We have a police officer en route with a severe head injury." *Rivera stopped Penski that day after he learned that she was driving her mother's vehicle without a license...*

My pace quickened as I entered the Emergency Center, after waving my badge in front of the sensors. When I arrived, I opened the door of the Trauma room and watched the team prepare for the injured man to arrive. A large staff of ten to twenty hovered behind the walls of the control "cockpit" and scattered throughout the room. Every person had something in hand and was carrying out a well-rehearsed role. I stood behind, in the "cockpit" watching the seamless preparation for a severely injured patient. This was my fourth month of training.

"This one's going to be really bad," the patient representative leaned over and whispered to me.

"Why is that?"

"The policeman has a head injury, a gunshot wound. Think you can handle it?"

"Sure," I responded tentatively, briefly reminding myself of the job I had to do, telling myself that this was *not* the time to even think about fainting. *Police said Penski told Rivera that she had family at the Summer Manor Apartment Complex in Devonshire and asked to be taken there.*

As I watched the team continue to prepare, the respiratory therapist at the head of the gurney looked up at me and practically yelled, "*You* know what this is for, don't you?" It really was more of a statement, not a question. I looked up rather startled, not realizing that he was talking to me. I nodded slowly and smiled, not even knowing what he was referring to.

We waited, adrenaline overflowing, jokes penetrating the air trying to assuage the flow. I was keeping a low profile, almost hiding behind the action. Sean, the patient rep, came up behind me and whispered in my ear, "Do you know what is being put on the table? It's a body bag. They don't expect this one to live." He turned to look me in the eye and had a mixture of sadness and understanding on his face. "You didn't know what John was talking about, did you?"

"No, I really didn't." I brushed the hair out of my eyes and decided to sit down in one of the available chairs. *When the two arrived at the apartment—and Rivera realized Penski had not been honest about having family there—they scuffled in the hallway and Rivera was shot dead, police said. Prosecutors contend Penski shot Rivera with his own gun.*

At first, I couldn't ever remember seeing a body bag. And then the memory slowly came into focus. "Mrs. Johnson, why don't you step outside your mother's room for just a moment. Maybe you could walk a bit down that hallway." She pointed around the corner. The tears were flowing. I had a difficult time putting one foot in front of the other. My husband had his arm around me. We walked down the hallway a few feet. There was nothing to say. She was gone. We stood there for what felt like forever. I turned to go back to her room as my husband grabbed me by the arm. "Not yet," he murmured. I pulled away from him and rounded the corner. That's when I saw it. Grey and zippered. My mom inside, covered and hidden. The body that had housed her, shamefully zipped into a heavy plastic bag. The body that had held me, surrounded me with warmth. The arms that pulled me back from danger. The hands that combed my long, tangled hair. The once-fattened tummy that we laughed at in the dressing room when we tried on clothes together, layers of fat rolling over her waistband, now lean and empty once and for all. And all of this, zipped into a bag.

"Are you OK, Chaplain?"

"Fine." I responded. A woman hurriedly moved among the team looking for the head emergency physician. "The officer will

Listening for Life

not be coming to this hospital," she said. "He was taken to the nearest hospital, DOA." Dead on arrival.

I stood up and stretched. It had been a rather long wait. I walked out into the hallway alone and leaned up against the wall. I wondered about this man's family. I later learned that he was married and had a thirteen-month-old daughter. Chances are they would never see his face again. Not once relegated to a body bag, especially since he had been shot in the head. The Rivera family had issued a statement at the time of the shooting, "The family is absolutely devastated by this tragedy…We do our best. We seem to break out crying at different times." The grandparents were saddened their granddaughter would probably be too young to remember her father.

Bodies. Bodies in bags. Practical? I suppose. Death can be messy. Death can smell bad. Death can be ugly, can distort, can mold into place a posture, gesture, or expression that does not reflect the person inside the body. Worthy carriers of a shell that tells a story? No.

A year later, I was sipping a coffee in the hospital cafeteria. It was a lonely night, quiet and calm. My eyes were drawn to the Christmas lights outside the hospital cafeteria windows. I startled as my pager went off, looked at the number, and got up to find a house phone. I called the number, and a nurse answered.

"Hi, this is the chaplain. I just received a page from you."

"Yes, we thought you should come up. A man just passed away, a priest. He was alone when he died but had already been anointed by a fellow priest."

"Is there any family to be called?"

"No, no one listed in his record."

His parents had already died. He had no aunts, uncles, brothers or sisters living, and of course, no children.

"I'll be right up."

"No hurry. We just thought he should be prayed over."

A few moments later, I arrived on the 5th floor of the Intensive Care Unit. The nurse looked up from her paperwork, stood, then came over to me as I walked over to her.

"His passing was so unexpected. He had started to get out of bed, said something about seeing Jesus and then laid back down and died." Her voice betrayed her deep caring. I put my hand on her shoulder for a moment, then turned to walk into his room.

I was shocked by what I saw. There was a body bag, already zipped, extending the length of the bed. I was to pray over a body bag? I stood by his bedside facing away from the doorway, tears streaming down my face. I said a prayer for him, knowing that he was at peace, even joyful in the arms of the One who knew and loved him best. I so wanted to unzip that bag. I wanted to see the face of the person I was praying for. I wanted to see the lines on his face, the tracks of the years around his eyes. I wanted to hold his hand that had blessed so many others throughout his lifetime. I should have asked the nurse to unzip the bag, but I did not. I was afraid. Maybe he could remain rather anonymous to me, a kind and compassionate priest without a face. I was afraid of taking the image home with me and pulling it out to look at it when I least wanted to. *She'll never know her father, which is so sad because he was such a tremendously outstanding man. On a lighter note…*

I placed the toothbrush back in the charging stand after rinsing it in the sink. I looked up at myself in the mirror—wrinkles deepening around my eyes and mouth. We are so quick to try to erase the tell-tale signs of living, I thought, the roadmap to the depths within. And then when we die, we immediately hide the evidence. Saddened by my discovery, I walked into the bedroom to get dressed for the day.

God on Both Sides of the Equation

There are times when listening will set off a wealth of personal memories within us. The news story about the policeman who died and the effect it had on his family began a string of memories, reaching deeply into my past few years, feelings emerging like wayward cats.

I often ask myself, *Am I able to listen to myself? Am I able to make sense out of the thoughts and feelings that surface or do I simply toss them away or put them on a shelf, hoping that I can close the door on them once and for all?*

When I took the time to listen to my heart, this is what I heard:

I had the confidence that I could handle a tough case but I was also unable to admit what I didn't know, and then, I finally came clean.

Memories of my mother's death poured through me, and I recall my vulnerability and trauma that day. What I saw will forever be with me.

I contemplated the worth of the person in the body bag and realized how valuable we all really are, even at the end.

I wondered about my inability to view the priest's face, afraid that I would carry his image in my memory. Was it really fear or was it repulsion, or maybe even my hesitancy to request a break in protocol?

I began to recognize and then relive the profound sadness that surrounds death and our hiding of the reality as soon as the person passes. I know there are good reasons for placing a body in a bag. But it seems so cold and impersonal.

Listening to Your Heart

- A situation can trigger past memories and emotions. Should this happen to you when caring for another, how might this be helpful to you in the moment?

- Are you able to listen to yourself? Not just your words, but your thoughts and feelings. Are you able to make sense of the thoughts that flow through you?
- Are you able to see yourself—a bird's eye view, if you will—and embrace both your strengths and weaknesses? What do you feel when you are able to do this?
- Might this ability change with age? Why do you think this is so?

CHAPTER 21
THE POWER OF PRESENCE

"Simply being with someone is difficult because it asks of us that we share in the other's vulnerability, enter with him or her into the experience of weakness and powerlessness, become part of the uncertainty, and give up control and self-determination."

—*Henri J. M. Nouwen*

My shift was nearing its end. I was filling in for the lead chaplain who had been out ill for several days, and I had documented numerous fruitful visits accordingly. Deciding that one more quick round through the Emergency Department, Trauma Room, and family waiting area would be a good way to end the day, I slowly walked through the main hallways looking for someone who might need attention.

All seemed at peace. I walked toward the family waiting room just off the ambulance entrance and spotted three young men sitting next to one another. All three had their heads bowed, staring as if they could penetrate beyond the floor tiles within their field of vision. As I approached, one of them looked up.

"May I help you with something? My name is Pastor Pat. I am one of the hospital chaplains. Is there anything you need?"

In slightly broken English, the young man said, "Yes. We are waiting to hear about our friend who was injured."

"Have you spoken with anyone yet?"

"Yes. Tamara said she would be right back."

Tamara was the patient representative assigned to the Emergency Department. She was the primary go-between and kept family members informed of the condition and whereabouts of their loved ones.

"Has she given you any information?"

"Well, we know he was brought here. We think he had a trucking accident. We were called in the middle of the night and drove in from Chicago. On our way from Chicago we got a call that our friend died." At this point the young man sitting to his far left began to weep silently, bending over as if he had been hit in the stomach.

"I am so sorry. Do you mind if I wait with you?"

"No. We would like that. This is Parvanda. This is Hamasa, and I am Faraz."

After a few moments of silence, I excused myself so I could talk with Tamara. I wanted to find out where things stood and what had happened. "I'll be right back."

Tamara emerged from the Trauma Room looking like she was on a mission.

"May I speak with you for just a moment?" I asked.

"I'll be right with you. I just have to give this paperwork to the clerk."

Tamara stepped behind me, and then I pulled her aside. "What is happening with the patient who was treated last night? The one who had the trucking accident. The three young men in the waiting room look terribly distraught."

"I'm trying to piece together what happened. So far, I know that the patient was driving a truck and had stopped in a truck stop to make an adjustment to the fittings between his two trailers. Something happened, and the trailers came together, crushing him between them." Her face did not betray any emotion. Tamara had to carry this visage with her everywhere she went. She had to be the face of reason and fact to those she cared for. Meanwhile, I know I was wincing and shaking my head.

"How awful!"

"Right now, I have a call in to the State Police, and I'm waiting to hear from the doctor who treated him last night."

"OK. I'll go sit with his friends."

"I'd appreciate that."

I reentered the room and took a seat next to Faraz. We sat in silence for what seemed like a very long time.

"I just saw him two days ago. I can't believe this has happened." He turned to his friends and spoke to them in a language I did not recognize.

"Tell me about him."

"Well, we are all about the same age. He was the oldest—twenty-three. We came to this country from Tajikistan. We all took trucking jobs so we could save money for college. We never intended to do this for long, but it pays very well."

"Have you known one another long?"

"Our families are close. I've known Abish for many years, but Parvanda knew Abish from the time they were babies," he nodded toward his friend on the far left who had been weeping. "I don't know how I am to tell his family."

"His parents are unaware of the accident?"

"Yes. We will probably tell our parents, and then they will go to his family and tell them." He stopped and took a deep breath with effort. "He was their only child."

I am fighting back tears as I imagine the scene when they are told. "Will they be able to come here for his body?"

"No. They couldn't afford that."

Never. Never seeing your child alive again. Not even able to see him in death. How does one cope with that? Sending him to America for a brighter future...and now, he is gone. There is no future.

"What is your faith tradition?"

Hamasa, the young man in the middle had not yet spoken except in his native language to his friends. He now took the lead. "We are Muslim." This is good for me to know. Good that I now know I cannot hug them. I learned this from my dear chaplain friend, Hau. I am old enough to be his mother, but as a female I cannot hug him, and I came very close to making this mistake not too long ago after seeing him on the floor of the hospital where I received half of my training.

I had been visiting my mother's cousin who had recently had a stroke and had visited with my first cousin at her bedside. Jennie and I had not seen one another for years. She had had bariatric surgery and had lost well over 150 pounds. She was contemplating having surgery to tighten up her skin which sagged mercilessly. We traded stories and then hugged. It was then that I caught a glimpse of Hau out of the corner of my eye. He saw me. I excused myself and walked quickly over to him holding out my arms—which he then brought together so that he could hold my hands. Alas, no hug for an old friend, but I do respect that and try to honor it. We talked briefly. He was having a hard time with tending to patients in palliative care, those who without the help of medical science, would have died. We parted, and I continue to think of him on and off. Hau is Sufi. I know that God is working powerfully in and through him.

I put my mothering instincts in check once again when I knew that these three men, young enough to be my sons, almost grandsons, were Muslim.

Tamara came into the room. "We have located the rest area where your friend was injured, and I have written it down for you on this paper so that you can go and explore. Also, there's a doctor here to talk with you."

All three young men raised their heads simultaneously. "This is Dr. Evans," said Tamara.

I stood up so she could take my seat. She carefully sat down, looking each man in the eyes one after another. "Your friend was brought in last night around 3:10 a.m. I was not the doctor who treated him, but I spoke with that doctor just a few minutes ago. When your friend was brought in, he did not have any vital signs. We performed CPR on him but were not successful. He was badly crushed, and we believe he died instantly. There was little or no suffering. We thought you should know that."

"Do you think someone else was involved? Do you think maybe he was hit over the head and put in between the trailers?" *Why is it that we always want to ascribe blame? If there was no one else around who could have caused this do we think God caused it?*

"We found no evidence of anything except the crushing. We will, of course, have to turn his body over to the medical examiner to do an autopsy."

Silence. And then, "That would be good." Conversation in their language was flowing freely now and wafting its way around the room.

"Do you have any more questions? Again, I'm so sorry for your loss."

More conversation. "Is he still here? Could we see him?"

Tamara responded, "Yes. I'll have to let the morgue know, and they will prepare him for viewing. Let me make some calls." She moved out of the room, as did the doctor. We were alone again, just the four of us. *What does one say at a time like this? Nothing. Silence is not only soothing, but it is necessary and allows for the processing of weighty grief that begins with shock.*

Tamara came back in about thirty minutes later. "The body is ready for viewing. Could you please gather up all of your belongings and come with me?"

We slowly stood and made our way to the door. Tamara took the lead, and I brought up the rear. This was so surreal, for me as well, as if the shock and denial had escaped from the room, following me and then entering into me. Like a virus it began spreading throughout my entire body, and I could feel its dull ache.

We walked down the long hallway to the elevator reserved for supplies, patients, and grieving families. When we got off, we encountered a security guard, a nurse, and an Emergency Department tech after we walked through a heavy metal door. They stood just outside of the viewing room. You see, in this hospital which hosts many significant crime victims, bodies must be viewed behind glass. No one is allowed to touch the body. The viewing room is tastefully decorated. There is an optional velvet curtain that can be closed before and after the viewing.

When we entered the room, the curtain was open. And there was the young victim, his body covered except for his head. His best friend, Parvanda, collapsed in grief when he came up to the glass. By this time, all three boys crowded around the window. Tears flowed freely. I stood in the background, placing my hand on each shoulder one after the other. And then I stood back and watched and prayed. *Ministry of presence. That is what I am giving these young men. There is nothing I can do to lessen this grief. The shock of seeing their friend behind glass, unbreathing, unseeing, immovable.*

I silently moved back into the hallway, fighting my own tears, knowing that dissolving into grief myself would not be helpful and yet knowing, too, that when the spiritual care person cries, it is human and bonding and real.

Moving back into the room, I checked for the usual concrete things—were there enough boxes of tissue? *No, there will never be enough tissue for this kind of grief.* I had accompanied another family to the viewing room first thing on Christmas Day. Their mother had pushed aside the suggestion that she go to the Emergency Department the day before, and then she had suffered a heart attack and died. She was fifty-three years old. Each family member had grieved differently—some keened loudly while others stood immobile and stoic. Some attended to other members of the family; others needed to be attended to. One daughter requested a wheelchair for her sister who was unable to stand up, she was so weighed down by her grief. The patient's sister shared with me that her son had committed suicide on Christmas Day just six years ago. *How much, O Lord, can one family bear?*

Seeing these three young men grieve shook me to my core. Their friend was the oldest, and they were having to face his death. Unexpected. Unfathomed. Unfair. The mother who had died had been ill for some time. This young man was strong, vibrant, and had plans for his future. He was hopeful, energetic, full of life. There is no comprehending this kind of loss.

So, we stood together as one before the glass. The boys cupped and raised their hands in prayer to Allah. Tamara was concerned that they were taking pictures with their iPhones. "No," I assured her. "They're praying." She had not been close enough to see. We waited, and then Faraz closed the curtain on his friend. Tamara took him aside and explained the process of finding a funeral home and having the funeral home call the hospital or medical examiner to obtain the body. She then directed them into the elevator. We exited and walked through the doors into the main lobby of the hospital. Parvanda was weeping loudly. Other visitors turned to look. Tamara led the way to the revolving doors, and I, once again, brought up the rear. We stopped a few feet away from the doors.

Tamara wished them well and said good-bye. I stood off to one side and then stepped up to say good-bye to each one. I took Hamasa by the hand. "God be with you."

I stepped up to Faraz. "If there is anything more we can do, please call."

As I moved toward Parvanda, he leaned into me, wrapping his arms around me briefly, then pulling back. *He is just a boy, Lord. He needs his mother.* I knew I could not be this for him, but I did tell him that I would be praying for him for many days and weeks to come. All three of them voiced their gratitude and disappeared through the revolving door.

My shift had ended almost an hour before. We are requested to adhere strictly to our shift times to provide order to the staff, and moving forward, to the overall health of the hospital. It did not matter to me that I might be docked that hour. The ministry of presence runs by a different clock, and I believe the administration knew that. I never did check my pay stub to see if I had been paid the extra hour.

God on Both Sides of the Equation

In my early years, I might have felt uncomfortable caring for someone of another faith. Throughout the years, however, I have learned that irrespective of our differences, we are all human, all loved by God, all in need of support when broken.

One of the wonderful things about chaplaincy training is that we learn to care for each person. We take into account and value but do not judge race, faith tradition (or no faith tradition), sexual orientation, political views, cultural heritage, socio-economic status or appearance. In my own Christian faith, I believe each person is of enormous value in God's sight, and my desire is to embrace this kind of love so I can shower it upon others.

What was especially beautiful in my interactions (mostly silence) was that, in the end, language and differences in faith were not a barrier to love and caring. I could honor a person simply because they are another human being.

Listening to Your Heart

- When was the last time you encountered someone very different from yourself? Were you able to be present with that person, listening without judging? What was going through your mind?

- When was the last time you sat in silence with another and resisted the need to fill the silence? Did you find this difficult?
- How does your belief system affect how you care for others? What helps you focus on the other person, even if you do not agree with what they are saying? Are you able to listen without comment or do you feel that you have to interject your "truth?"

EPILOGUE
OUR MARK

Wanderers, for good or ill we leave our mark
Whenever we land, whatever we touch.

—*Luci Shaw*

Almost fifteen years have passed since I wrote the first story in this book. I would never have thought to do this except that one night, before I succumbed to sleep and after a meaningful encounter with a patient earlier in the day, I heard these words: "Write these things down." My mind flitted back to the John of Revelation, and setting aside feelings of unworthiness, I took these words seriously and began to write down the vignettes that held meaning for me.

From the very inception of this book, listening was paramount. I began listening for life in others and in myself. Listening for God in the middle of my challenging days became a blessed routine. Thus, hearing God's voice within me at the start of my chaplaincy journey and then being given the time at the end of this journey to write about these encounters became a gift beyond my imagination! I was beginning to put together the insight that God was and is on "both sides of the equation," working in the person receiving the gift of love and working in me at the same time.

As I ponder this tender ministry of chaplaincy, I am able to see that each of us has left our mark on those we have served. Some will remember us. Some will not. But our work stands on its own. Our touch, the sound of our prayers and the questions we gently asked will have a ripple effect. Our ability to listen and to be present in the silence allowed those in the room to feel and think on their own. The space gave them a chance to grow and to piece together their own lives in the present and moving forward. Many were able to allow confidence to build within them. Some who had shied away from grief, entered the process with courage. Many shared stories that helped them to make sense of their lives. We helped them tie up the loose ends.

There were times when a loved one needed someone with whom to be angry, and we were right there to field that anger. Many needed someone to share fantastic stories with, hoping they would be believed, and they were. We honored their perception of reality. Many who cried looked up and found tears on our faces as we joined them in their sadness. We were sometimes able to stem the tide of loneliness and unbelonging because we accepted people right where they were without judgement.

My hope and prayer is that you can now see your own life in these terms. You, too, have left your mark—wherever God has taken you. Like us, you have made mistakes and have regretted lost opportunities. Even so, your love has flowed over so many people, and others have been changed because of it. Never minimize what you have done and given. You may never know the impact of these gifts until this life is over.

I hope you have learned how listening affects those who need to be cared for. I also hope you continue to listen to the voice of

God within you and that you listen to yourself in order to know yourself better, to care for yourself, and to forgive yourself.

Life for others is fuller because of you. Always remember that! Life is in the listening. Listen closely.

ACKNOWLEDGEMENTS

My first note of gratitude goes to all of those patients and families who shared their lives with me. Little did they know at the time that I was benefiting just as much as they were. God was using our words to speak to one another, bringing insight and growth to all of us, including you.

Thanks then goes to Alice Crider who made suggestions and did substantial editing to the manuscript. As a certified life coach, editor, and all around encourager, she made the process easier than it could have been. I could always count on her to make relevant suggestions and answer any questions I had about the entire publishing process. She gave me courage and direction and helped me to think "outside the box."

My fellow spiritual director and therapist, Nancy Sparrow, also gave me incredible insight into the substance of my manuscript. Because of our similar training, I knew I could count on her to find inconsistencies or flaws in my thinking. She helped me broaden my terminology to be more inclusive and assisted me in making my questions less directive and more thoughtful.

On the front end, I depended on several individuals to do a first reading of a few chapters so I had input into defining my audience: Steve Hankal, Lyn Dunkerly, Barb Polsgrove, and Doug Adams.

During the writing of this book, there were so many who encouraged me. I want to thank Rev. Dr. Patricia Chunn, with whom I became companions on the chaplain journey. She has been so generous in her compliments and support. I specifically want to mention Beverly Beltramo, DMin, BCC, Director of Spiritual Care at Ascension, Michigan. She was instrumental in my certification as a chaplain. I was also given the honor of working under her twice in different hospital systems. Her tender care and inspiration greatly contributed to my self-confidence in finishing this book.

Much thanks and gratitude goes to my publishing team from Emerge: Richard Robinson, Christian Ophus, and Julie Werner. I especially appreciated Richard's persistence and tenacity on the front end, Christian's creativity as we decided on cover art, and Julie's expertise in managing the project, holding everything together. Between us, we experienced COVID restrictions, illness, an automobile accident, bypass surgery, snow and more! We finally made it to the finish line!

NOTES

1. Fox, John. "When Someone Deeply Listens to You." 1995. Pollycastor.com/2018/09/26/when-someone-deeply-listens-to-you-poem-by-john-fox/ (Accessed 2020)

Introduction
1. The quotation made by the "veteran of Weight Watchers" is a popular song, *"Pick Yourself Up"* composed in 1936 by Jerome Kern, with lyrics by Dorothy Fields. The song was written for the film *Swing Time* (1936), where it was introduced by Fred Astaire and Ginger Rogers.

Chapter 1
1. Norris, Kathleen. *The Cloister Walk*. (Riverhead Books, 1997) p. 323.
2. Jung, Carl. *Carl Jung Quotes*. (*Wikiquotes*, 20 August 2019) *en.wikiquote.org/wiki/Carl_Jung*. Jung used this quotation often but it is attributed to him in error. This is actually a statement that Jung discovered among the Latin writings of Desiderius Erasmus, who declared the statement had been an ancient Spartan proverb. Jung popularized it, having it inscribed over the doorway of his house, and upon his tomb.

Chapter 3
1. Carmichael, Amy. *Thou Givest, They Gather.* (CLC Publications, 2010) p. 265-66.

Chapter 4
1. Hellerman, Joseph. "A Family Affair," Christianity Today. Volume 54, Number 5. May 28, 2010, p. 43.
2. Norris, Kathleen. *The Cloister Walk.* (Riverhead Books, 1997) p. 346.
3. Williams, Cecil and Laird, Rebecca. *No Hiding Place.* (Harper Collins, 1992) p. 22. Williams was the pastor of Glide Memorial Church in San Francisco. He noted in his book: "When people come to Glide, we don't ask them if they are atheists, Methodist, or Buddhists. We ask them what their names are and how they're doing."

Chapter 5
1. Source unknown.
2. Mason, Mike. *Practicing the Presence of People: How We Learn to Love.* (Colorado Springs, CO: Waterbrook Press, 1999) p.260.
3. Mason, Mike. *Practicing the Presence of People: How We Learn to Love.* (Colorado Springs, CO: Waterbrook Press, 1999) p.261.

Chapter 6
1. Johnson, Patricia Taylor. *Jorell* (poem), 2007.

Chapter 7
1. Grogan, John. *Marley and Me.* (New York: HarperCollins, 2005) p. 282.

Chapter 8
1. Edwards, Kim. *The Memory Keeper's Daughter.* (New York: Penguin Books, 2006) p. 122.

Chapter 9

1. *Lamentations 3:1* (Verse 1 of an Hebrew acrostic poem. Each stanza begins with the successive letters of the Hebrew alphabet.)
2. Barth, Karl. *The Epistle to the Romans,* paraphrased.
3. Lewis, C.S. *The Problem of Pain.* As quoted in "C.S. Lewis on the Problem of Pain" by Jana Harmon, Knowing & Doing, C.S. Lewis Institute, 12 Aug 2012. www.cslewisinstitute.org/C_S_Lewis_on_the_Problem_of_Pain_page3
4. Augustine of Hippo, *City of God.* This quotation was popularized by Dr. Gerald May who wrote *Addiction and Grace.* May did not give us an exact original source. The best way to locate the precise quotation would be to search the original in Latin, but I was unable to locate a person who tackled this.
5. Lewis, C.S. The Official Website of C.S. Lewis, *The Problem of Pain.* www.cslewis.com/the-problem-of-pain/March, 2019.

Chapter 10

1. Suffield, Kittie Louise. Lyrics: *"Little is Much When God is in It."* (1924).

Chapter 11

1. Keltner, Dacher. *The Science of Touch,* quoting Michelangelo di Lodovico Buonarroti Simoni. "Hands On Research, The Science of Touch." *Greater Good Magazine.* September 29, 2010.

Chapter 12

1. Stoney, J.B. *"Letters on Subjects of Interest," "My Peace." (Third Series.* London: G. Morrish.) p. 28.

Chapter 13

1. Withers, Bill. Music and lyrics: *Lean on Me* (Sussex Records, 1972).
2. Lovland, Rolf and Graham, Brendon. (2002). *You Raise Me Up.* (Recorded by J. Groban on *Closer.*) (2003).

Chapter 14
1. Singh, Sadhu Sundar. *At the Master's Feet* (Fleming H. Revell, 1922) p. 45.

Chapter 15
1. Jung, Carl. Quotable Quotes (Goodreads 2020) www.goodreads.com/quotes/248440-through-pride-we-are-ever-deceiving-ourselves-but-deep-down (Accessed 2020)

Chapter 16
1. Gardner, E'yen A. *Humbly Submitting to Change: The Wilderness Experience.* (Printed Word Publishing, 2008).

Chapter 17
1. Angelou, Maya. Quotable Quotes (Goodreads, accessed 2019) www.goodreads.com/quotes/5141700-i-ve-learned-that-no-matter-what-happens-or-how-bad (Accessed 2020)

Chapter 18
1. Franciscan. *Blessing of the Pets.* www.saintpats.org/parish/bless-pets-feast-st-francis-assisi/
    The blessing of pets and animals is often celebrated on October 4, the feast of St. Francis of Assisi, or on a Sunday near that date. ... The blessing of each animal, by name, means that health, healing and life are being mediated from God for the benefit of the animal in its relationship with its human partners. (Accessed 2020)
2. Nouwen, Henri. *With Open Hands.* This concept was taken from Chapter 5: Prayer and Revolution, pp. 59-76.

Chapter 19
1. Kadish, Rachel. *The Weight of Ink.* (Mariner Books, 2017) p. 55.

Chapter 20
1. Ferguson, Marilyn. *The Art of Personal Effectiveness* (Weiser Books, 2005) p. 35.

Chapter 21
1. McNeill, Donald P., Morrison, Douglas A., and Nouwen, Henri. *Compassion: A Reflection on the Spiritual Life.* (Image, 2006) p. 12

Epilogue
1. Shaw, Luci. *Harvesting Fog: Poems by Luci Shaw.* "Camping, California Coast." (Pinyon Publishing, 2010) p. 58.

Made in the USA
Monee, IL
17 September 2023

42903235R00106